WILL THE REAL YOUNG AMERICA PLEASE STAND UP?

WILL THE REAL
PLEASE

*The until-now silent, youthful
majority's call for a return
to the traditional principles
that made this country great*

YOUNG AMERICA STAND UP?

Mark Evans

Stackpole Books

WILL THE REAL YOUNG AMERICA PLEASE STAND UP?
Copyright © 1973 by
THE STACKPOLE COMPANY

Published by
STACKPOLE BOOKS
Cameron and Kelker Streets
Harrisburg, Pa. 17105

Printed in the U.S.A.

Library of Congress Cataloging in Publication Data

Evans, Mark.
    Will the real young America stand up?

    1. Young adults--United States. 2. United States
--Social conditions--1960-   3. Radicalism--United
States. I. Title.
HQ799.7.E8   301.43'15'0973   73-12376
ISBN 0-8117-1897-2

Table of Contents

Preface

As an author who prefers to express himself through ideas rather than through a first-person narrative, I shall include no personal references in the forthcoming pages. However, I believe it necessary to explain briefly my reasons for devoting considerable time and space to a discussion of the young men and women of my generation.

During the past decade, America has been obsessed with youth. No aspect of daily living has been free from influence by a set of customs, mannerisms, sounds, attitudes, and prejudices which are generally identified with all young Americans. Some persons refer to this movement as the "counterculture"; I choose to call it the "youth cult."

Although millions of Americans have been demonstrably hostile to this cult, large numbers of highly vocal citizens have taken the opposite view. They purport to "understand" the trials and tribulations of young America. They advertise their receptive attitudes toward "young ideas" and dismiss dissenters as antiquated specimens, too ignorant or unsophisticated to progress with the times.

The philosophy and literature of the youth cult have been confused and erratic. Books explaining the changes that have affected America during the last fifteen years range from the primitive obscenities of the campus radicals to sophisticated academic studies. Sociologists and psychologists approach these problems with a scholarly, clinical attitude, while commercial writers strive to inform the public in the most shocking ways possible of the latest traditions which are to be discarded in the name of progress.

All of these books (and their widely publicized authors) have one quality in common: they assume without question that there is a single "young" viewpoint to which sophisticated young adults generally subscribe. They equate change with progress and morality with convenience; they are permeated by inaccuracies and superficial, simplistic conclusions. Most of all, they literally deny the existence of those members of the younger generation who do not support their theories.

By way of introduction I must add a personal note. I do not have to prove my youth or rationalize my own capacity for achievement. I have no axe to grind, no ideological mission, no personal vendetta to conclude. But apologists for the youth cult do not speak for me. They do not speak for the thousands of young men and women who, like me, have survived academic inequities, bureaucratic stupidity, and often brutal assaults upon our ideals because we believed that the world could be made a better place through individual accomplishment and mature responsibility.

The most thoughtful and passionate of our youth believe in excellence, in morality, and in values. The youth cult is diametrically opposed to all of these elements. We have been compelled to witness the birth of a perverse and warped culture, presumably representing our generation, aided and abetted by an absurd group of middle-aged adults frightened beyond belief at the prospect of growing old.

At the heart of the youth cult is a distorted, twisted standard. Honors, adulation, and the mantle of respectability are reserved for those who achieve the ultimate in mediocrity, immorality, and hypocrisy. Those of us who believe in the viability of traditional values are described as "irrelevant" to our own generation.

History has proven that men and ideas may both be measured by what they stand for, rather than what they stand against. Those who see the events of the 1960's and 1970's as a great step forward do us a disservice. They make it difficult, if not impossible, for constructive, positive revitalization of those customs and institutions that are the bulwark of freedom and a civilized society.

We are not satisfied with the world. We are not complacent in the face of war, poverty, disease, or decay. We want the same things our parents wanted, the same goals to which man has eternally aspired. Unfortunately, we stand between two extremes in society. One extreme desires the status quo; the other seeks to enact change for the sake of change, change at any price. After all the philosophical analysis, sociological speculation, academic jargon, metaphysical expostulation, and epistemological theory has ended, what does the youth cult offer us? A society in which the singularly important components are drug addiction, indiscriminate sex, dirt, filth, ignorance, illiteracy, and cultural Yahooism; in short, verbal niceties are employed to defend slobbism.

We believe that the greatest threat facing our country today is the segment of middle-aged adults who seek to turn over our culture and our society to those members of our generation who are least qualified to sustain it and most likely to destroy it. A responsible youth today has few places to go. He is not welcome in the groves of academe, where radicals are greeted and reformers are ignored. He is not welcome in the creative arts, where standards of taste have become so commercialized that a lack of talent is often considered a prime advantage in the prognosis for success. He may be considered eligible for the business world, but only if he subscribes to predetermined concepts of "youthfulness" in his manners, dress, and speech.

We are told constantly that America's hope is in its youth. This may well be the case, but only if we do not vulgarize the term "youth" to encompass anyone who happens to have lived for a prescribed number of years. America's real leaders have tried to devote themselves to learning, to preparation, to study, and most important, to self-development. America's hope is its forgotten young Americans who do not subscribe to the youth cult.

Our generation needs leaders, not political schemers; demands accomplishment, not the debunking of excellence. It requires values of substance, not moral erosion. It is ironic that apologists for the youth cult, so ready and eager to "understand," to "communicate," to "listen," and not incidentally to "imitate" and to "conform," have made our world all the harder. In their world, the unwashed ignoramus becomes the hope for the future; the responsible young man or woman becomes a curiosity, an oddity; and a vestigial manifestation of a society in its decline.

When academicians try to portray us as custodians of the status quo, they insult our intelligence, mock our values, ridicule our imagination, and do all of these things in the name of "understanding youth." Young Americans everywhere may worry about their futures, their families, their work at school or in their careers. They are often compelled to ask: "Is there a place for me?" When they see ostensibly mature adults ready to turn society upside-down to cater to a select element of youth which proclaims itself the hope of America, they are compelled to believe that the answer is "No."

In recent months, Americans have started to discuss the excesses of the 1960's, expressing hope that the new decade of the 1970's will represent an era of new hope. Some young men and women are saying that the self-styled "revolution" which allegedly reached our college campuses was a mistake; they are now looking for some other way to effect change, a constructive, positive, meaningful way to re–examine their lives and their relationships to each other.

Some young Americans are tired of being dismissed as irrelevant, conservative, old-fashioned, and out-of-date. Some middle-aged Americans are tired of being subjected to ridicule and abuse because they approach their children as leaders, not followers. Both these groups of Americans are tired of hippies, Yippies, and malcontents. They are tired of a sub-culture that cannot survive without depending on drugs or stimulants. They are tired of rock musicians, poets, artists and writers who are so totally lacking in even a single shred of ability that they compelled Ernest Hemingway to call this "The Millennium of the Untalented." They are tired of seeing dirty, filthy, unwashed slobs being glorified as heroes. They are tired of a culture whose vocabulary demands vulgarity, coarseness, and obscenity. They are no longer able to tolerate the demise of taste or the apotheosis of slobbism. Most of all, they will refuse to countenance the efforts of those poor, misguided adults who should know better to offer this new culture as the only alternative for America. They will totally reject efforts to proclaim a new society which is established by tearing down the government, the schools, the churches, the families, and the institutions which are the very life-blood of a healthy nation. They seek a return to morals, values, and a meaningful culture in the most sophisticated sense. They realize that an X-rated film, an underground newspaper, and a uniform of dirty clothing does not make a philosopher or a moral sage any more than the ability to wave the flag makes one a patriot. They will turn back the philosophical assault on the home, the family, and a real sense of values. They recognize the exciting, dynamic, positive alternatives that do exist today. They seek a return to common sense in America. They know the youth cult is not the only alternative because they are the real alternative.

I have written this book for them.

I.

The Generation Gap: Casting in Stereotype

If any subject may be said to arouse an emotional response in the hearts and minds of men it is today's youth. Americans may be found who subscribe to every possible faith, creed, or personal philosophy. But it is difficult to find any American who has not addressed himself at one time or another in the recent past to the question of our young people: where they have been, where they are, and most important of all, where they are going. Mention the youth of America in your local barbershop, grocery store, or police station. Remind a successful corporate executive or a labor-union leader about his children. Question your clergyman or high-school principal about the activities of the younger generation. The spectrum of responses will be infinite and contradictory. Undoubtedly, at least one person will suggest that young Americans are tools of the devil, bent upon their own destruction (and everyone else's), eager to earn a place for themselves in the raging fires of hell. Another popular response is that the young, referred to vaguely as "the kids," are not to blame for our current political and social difficulties, and that if the mature-adult community will only abandon its hostile or lethargic state, the young will lead it out of the wilderness.

Obviously, such emotional responses do little in the way of explaining why many young people behave as they do; true understanding requires penetrating, in-depth analysis. Occasionally, someone tries to interpret America's growing youth culture, proposing to explain the whys and wherefores of young Americans,

13

with emphasis on discerning a logical pattern of events that may render a new, subtle coherence to occurrences that have seemed otherwise incomprehensible.

The decade of the 1960's was a time of radical change for America. At one time, politicians used to suggest that the flag, motherhood, and apple pie were subjects which could never be publicly criticized. But during the 1960's, every imaginable taboo in our daily lives was challenged, if not altered. Because these changes occurred on a gradual basis, some social observers were not quick to recognize that the combination of all these elements together could result in a new political, social, and cultural revolution. Many of the ways in which society has changed are so well-known as to make their retelling unnecessary. Ultimately, the culture, dress, attitudes, music, and drugs with which many young persons identified became known as the "counterculture." The counterculture had its own literature, its own music and films, its own political activities, and its own heroes. Today, many Americans have forgotten about the counterculture. The Vietnam War has moved from the military to the political spectrum; the college campuses have quieted down; the 1970's seem, superficially, more stable, more calm, and we seem headed back toward normalcy.

The illusion is desirable but unjustified. In the 1970's, many of the influences of the counterculture are still alive. But they have moved directly into the mainstream of society. One reason for the change is that many influences of the 1960's youth revolution have been welcomed, promoted, and defended by a large, articulate, and highly influential group of citizens. These men and women often describe themselves as liberal and open-minded; they say that they believe that this new revolution, the expression of the new youth culture, will be a peaceful non-violent cultural upheaval which will change our lives and our values simultaneously and for the better.

These men and women are active in the educational world, in publishing, and in the news media; they all affect our communications, the means whereby Americans learn what other Americans are thinking. For the most part, they have portrayed our social ills in terms of a generation gap. In a gross oversimplification, they have chosen to identify a number of social and political attitudes with young people; in a neat and curious dichotomy, they divide the rest of society into two groups: those who understand the kids and those who don't.

The result of this occurrence is that many Americans have come to accept stereotypes and pre-fashioned images and definitions. The generation gap has been portrayed as a struggle between our "young people" and their middle-aged supporters, who want to change the whole direction of our society, and the old-fashioned, antiquated men and women who are too unsophisticated or narrow-minded to appreciate these changes.

Because of this emphasis on the generation gap, many Americans have proceeded to draw conclusions about the younger generation. Ideas are labeled "young" or "old." Much of our society remains unaware that many young Americans do not subscribe to the ideas which are set forth as representing the younger generation. The existence of a large segment of America's young people has been ignored by professors, writers, publishers, sociologists, and the news media. Why has this happened?

The error lies in the failure to recognize that the generation gap is not really a struggle between the young and the old, but rather between two value systems. For obvious reasons, one value system has chosen to wrap itself in the mantle of progress, change, and youthful idealism. It is difficult to oppose ideas which are advanced under this banner; it is socially unfashionable and one runs the risk of being called a variety of names, all of which are most unpleasant. It is easier to praise the new youth revolution as a splendid example of twentieth-century progress.

Many Americans do not realize that the idea of the generation gap is a direct result of an unconscious conspiracy between some well-meaning but thoroughly misguided individuals. Whenever the subject of conspiracy is raised, the person who calls attention to the subject is ridiculed. Admittedly, there are those who think that there are Communists hiding under every bed, and their efforts to wake up America seem more laughable or pathetic than serious. But this conspiracy, as previously stated, has been unconscious. It is a difficult and bizarre occurrence to describe.

For the last several decades, a large segment of the professors, liberal by their own definition, have expounded their political and social views. Some of these men are distinguished scholars in a specific field; some do not have the common sense to come in out of the rain. Their academic credentials may be impressive and tend to blur this fact. The professors have taught young men and women who have gone on to become journalists, reporters, sociologists, writers, and politicians; many have participated in various aspects of the news media. These individuals in the communications field spend their time commenting on American society, and making their ideas known to the public. The effect tends to be cyclical: the professors teach their students who later write books. The books are reviewed by critics who are favorable to the views of the professors. The news media men read the books, with their favorable critical reviews, and report on the events they see taking place in the nation. Being human, they often allow their personal views to color their reports. The professors listen to the news reports, which have been written by journalists, some of whom appear to investigate on a subjective level, finding those news stories that reinforce their views.

The cycle starts all over again when the professors react to the news stories by reinforcing their views. These men and women talk to each other, read the same books, share the same ideas. They pride themselves on being intellectual. They are often extremely articulate to the point of glibness. This tends to confuse those who do not share their verbal facility but who feel uncomfortable with their arguments. In turn, these men and women go around in an intellectual circle. They thrive on pseudo-intellectual snobbery, because they all read the "best books," belong to the "best political groups," study the attitudes of the "most brilliant thinkers." Many of these men and women live and work in the East, provoking some bitter resentment against an Eastern clique. They often seem oblivious to the prevailing views of Americans in the Midwest and South. But it would be a great mistake to portray this problem in geographic terms. Every section of the country has its share of ignoramuses, well-educated or otherwise.

In the 1960's, these men and women exercised a profound influence on our society by persuading us of the nature of the youth-cult revolution. They failed to recognize the true nature of the "generation gap"; in fact, books, ideas, and activities that did not reinforce their preconceived views were ignored or ridiculed. Now in the 1970's, these same men and women are advising us to "learn from our mistakes of the 1960's." They have learned little themselves.

Before writing this book, I was advised by experts on the publishing field that the critics and reviewers are all on the other side; the book will never have a chance, even though it tells the truth. The pseudo-intellectual and critical élite of this country do not want to be forced to look at the reality of the counterculture or its more respectable assimilation into mainstream society.

There are many in the United States today who pride themselves on their objectivity, but they thrust their heads into the ground when confronted with the fact that many young people do not subscribe to the youth cult or its promoters in any age bracket.

In this book, the reader is invited to join the author in exploring the counterculture of the 1960's and to examine its influence on the 1970's. We shall quickly learn that the revolution of our young people is not representative of our young people at all, but of a segment of all generations. It is a bizarre story in which America's values are turned upside-down. In many ways, this nation's upheavals have resembled Alice's Wonderland. Most of the central figures in this story wear bizarre clothing and behave in strange ways. Some are irreverent, and like the Cheshire Cat, are grinning and smirking for no reason at all. Some, like the Duchess who continues sneezing while pouring pepper into a baby's soup, continue to ferment trouble and agitate for changes; they do not realize that these changes are misguided and often evil. There are many academicians, who seem to have borrowed Lewis Carroll's "curriculum" of Reeling, Writhing, and all the parts of Arithmetic: ambition, distraction, uglification, and derision. There is a villain, of course, vaguely defined as the Establishment, and a chorus of shrill voices screaming, "Off with their heads."

America, in short, has been conducting a Mad Tea Party. The invited guests have been too bewildered to understand what has happened. Like Alice, they are still trying to find their way home.

Today, our country has survived the initial onslaught of the youth-cult revolution. But we are greatly changed by the events of the last few years. It is difficult to find a sense of reality, especially since a large segment of society believes that our national ills are indicative of a generation gap. They do not realize that acceptance of the cultural revolution represents a surrender of our national identity, not to our "young people" but to a segment of society which is incapable of governing itself, let alone solving everyone else's problems.

Many of those who have been led astray by the Mad Tea Party have been literate, well-educated, and in the scientific sense, highly intelligent. But their theories and perspectives have been fashioned so as to produce conclusions which are totally opposite of those justified. Many of us care about America. We care about its future, and about the young Americans who will be its leaders someday. We care too much to be satisfied with half-truths, illogical conclusions, distortion of some facts, and deliberate ignorance of others which fail to support a preconceived theory of our social condition. In the following pages, we shall observe the errors in the ways of those who welcome the social revolution of our youth culture, and consider possible alternatives to this revolution, which is capable of destroying much that is good and true in American society.

It is important to remember that a great difference exists between recognizing that problems exist and proposing valid solutions for those problems. We may correctly identify a social ill, but propose a solution that would fail to provide a cure. In some instances, the "cure" may do more damage than the illness. Another possibility is the failure to recognize the cause of a problem or to draw conclusions from a premise that is incorrect in the first place.

In examining this youth-cult revolution of the 1960's and 1970's, we must become skilled in the art of perceiving redefinitions. Words often suggest images; one reason for the confusion that exists in society today is the tendency to make judgments based upon the use of labels. For example, the words "young" or "old" are often used synonymously with "progressive" or "anachronistic." When the public read Jim Bouton's book, *Ball Four*, they were surprised to discover that baseball players engaged in a variety of activities involving liquor and sex. "Baseball" conveyed another image to the sports fans, and the image seemed incongruous. When non-Catholics think of a priest, they often think of a figure resembling the character of Father O'Malley, as portrayed by Bing Crosby in the film, *Going My Way*. The term "professor" conveys an image of scholarly wisdom, civic responsibility, and academic expertise. High-school newspapers convey the image of football rallies and cheerleaders and senior proms.

Discussions about the views of young people are often tempered by labels and definitions. It has become fashionable to pigeonhole citizens according to age, sex, race, and political persuasion. The most brutal of military despots will not acknowledge that he is a dictator. Instead, he tries to perpetuate the myth that his power is derived from the people, and that he exercises his authority because of popular will. The fact that a man speaks out against war or poverty or in favor of civil liberties or freedom means only that he favors or opposes ideas which are generally accepted by all civilized men. It does not mean that his conclusions are justified or that he even uses these terms to mean the same states of affairs that his detractors do.

Curiously, all nations publicly profess their desires for peace, indicating that the governments of these nations have very different definitions of behavior that is conducive to real peace as defined by everyone. It is always amusing to hear politicians in an election year making fearless statements condemning such universally recognized evils as floods or earthquakes, because these politicians try to make themselves appear heroic.

An old and widely used practice in the offices of Hollywood directors is the procedure known as "typecasting." This term refers to the use of a predetermined stereotype image in determining which actors should be hired for which roles. For example a casting director may assume that all doctors are tall, thin, middle-aged, with gray hair. Whenever he has to cast the role of a doctor, this director automatically turns to men who fit his predetermined notion of what a doctor should look like. The fact that hundreds of physicians do not fit this image is no concern to the director. An actor may be typecast because he is only identified with specific roles.

Let us examine some commonly used labels. We shall quickly see how terms are often confused, and how we can persuade ourselves that up is down and right is wrong.

The hosts of our Mad Tea Party have assumed that Americans can be divided into neat categories. Some citizens, we are told, are "conservative." They want to return to an imaginary yesterday in which America was a nation of small towns and simple virtues. They select their political candidates on the basis of morality; they yearn for the past, days of reliance on private business, abolition of welfare, and reawakening of vigilance against domestic subversion. In contrast to the backward conservatives, we are able to find the "liberals." By their own definition, the liberals are better educated, more sophisticated, more open-minded than conservatives.

The classic commercial images of conservatives and liberals are the television characters, Archie Bunker and Maude Findlay. Both characters were developed through the production endeavors of Norman Lear. Both characters have become part of American folklore through the success of "All in the Family" and "Maude" on television. Archie Bunker is a funny, ridiculous caricature, skillfully portrayed by Carroll O'Connor. But Archie is unappealing, ignorant, and bigoted. We may laugh at "All in the Family," but we don't want to be like Archie. Even the real Archies laugh at the Bunkers because they don't see themselves reflected in Archie's image. "Maude" was initially announced as a satire of the die-hard liberal. Allegedly, the show would portray the other side of the coin. C. H. Simonds, in a column entitled "The Honesty Trap" sees through the façade with this observation. "Loud-mouthed, featherheaded, flatulent, enuretic though she may be, Maude is by-golly on the side of the angels, she's right to have the abortion, Peace Now. Counterbalance to Archie Bunker, my foot. Come Message Time, Archie and all he stands for (bigotry, narrowness, insensitivity; also patriotism, hard work, traditional morality) are usually shot down in flames."

These last elements, patriotism, hard work, and traditional morality, are publicly identified with ignorant, ill-educated bigotry (Archie) or stupidity (his wife Edith). In turn, "Maude" continues to perpetuate these images by pretending to satirize the liberals and social reformers while trumpeting their ideological causes.

Not everyone who believes in hard work or traditional morality is an ill-educated bigot with little ability to perceive the great philosophical or moral issues of our time. The fact that intelligent, highly literate conservatives find themselves on the same side as Archie Bunker on some issues does not mean that they are unsophisticated ignoramuses, any more than the critical élite's meek, misty-eyed tolerance of Marxism or anarchy means that members of the press corps are personally Communists or anarchists.

Advocates of the youth cult like Archie as a foil. He's a wonderful target, because many Americans will check their common sense at the door to make themselves feel progressive (unlike Archie!). The image of a plodding, ignorant, corrupt, bigoted Establishment is a convenience for the hosts of our Mad Tea Party. They offer a steady diet of the youth cult, with the veiled threat that unless we want to be as stupid as the Bunkers, we'd better sit down and have some tea.

Let us examine some typical redefinitions. Progress, we are told, is redefined as change. If we accept this neat notion, we assume that any idea is valid because it is new. But change is not synonymous with progress. A tornado may "change" a town by levelling it; this does not imply constructive alteration by any means.

Russell Kirk has expressed this idea eloquently in his *The Conservative Mind*: "Recognition that change and reform are not identical, and that innovation is a devouring conflagration more often than it is a torch of progress. Society must alter, for slow change is a means of conservation, like the human body's perpetual renewal; but Providence is the proper instrument for change, and the test of a statesman is his cognizance of the real tendency of Providential social forces."

The plight of the working man is eloquently retold, with one small alteration. The workers' struggle is based upon conditions which existed at the time of Samuel Gompers. We cannot evaluate the relationship between modern corporations and the AFL–CIO as governed by George Meany's administration in the same terms. But since it suits the political motives of the New Left to treat labor relations in these terms, the advocates of the New Politics are not to be restrained.

Once we become accustomed to these redefinitions, we can easily recognize how arguments can become distorted. For example, the television and news media devote considerable attention to the women's liberation movement. More often than not, their viewpoint is presented as the "woman's view." No qualifications are needed. The critical élite who read the best books and communicate with the most brilliant intellectuals realize that there is only one woman's view. The other women are Edith Bunkers.

Mrs. Helen B. Andelin, a Santa Barbara mother of eight, wrote a book called *Fascinating Womanhood.* Major publishers rejected the book because obviously it was unrelated to the cultural mainstream as seen by the women's liberationists. Mrs. Andelin proposed that, "A woman can gain true happiness in marriage by placing the husband's happiness as a primary goal." Mrs. Andelin's book, which counseled women to cultivate femininity and stay away from the business world, sold over 200,000 copies. But Mrs. Andelin had to publish her book through her own company because the publishers were being "open-minded" about the woman's view, the only one they recognize.

When 150 members of the American Society for Divorced Men picketed the Civic Center Plaza in Chicago, the *New York Times* was disinterested. The newspaper gave the men a small paragraph in the back of the paper; only men favoring women's liberation could get front-page coverage.

This attitude toward women is similar to the view of young people. Only those young people whose views approximate those of the critical élite are recognized with any validity.

Consider some specific examples of controversies relating to the generation gap. Imagine that you encountered these issues without any preconceived knowledge of the redefinition game that is played by our social advisors.

A high-school newspaper is published by some students who are registered at the high school. The newspaper is not the official school publication, but is distributed on campus by these students on their own. The principal or the school board objects to the newspapers, and plans are made to ban them from the campus. An outcry is raised; the school administration is foolish and unimaginative. They have bowed to pressure from a parent who vaguely resembles Archie Bunker. The American Civil Liberties Union steps into the battle. We hear demands for free speech and quotations from Thomas Jefferson.

Superficially, the image we receive is typical of the generation gap: our "young people" being stifled by old-fashioned adults who are too backward to appreciate their creativity or their free spirits.

Now before you join the bandwagon and begin shouting about what the Establishment is doing to "our children," examine the following description of the high-school underground newspaper that caused the controversy.

This newspaper contained every variety of four-letter word; it abounded in obscenities. One similar newspaper devoted considerable attention to student demonstrations. Special attention was devoted to relationships with the police, including such topics as "How to behave when a cop frisks you." Advice of this kind is common: "Local cops and the FBI may question you. Don't answer! You have a right to remain silent." The article concludes with references to students who should prepare to wear helmets, and expect tear gas or mace. Exercising their free speech, the students go on to declare, "Don't bring your address book; if you are busted, the cops will get the names of all your friends."

One "student newspaper" issues its demands: open admission to colleges, no suspensions or expulsions, freedom of speech, freedom of the press, establishment of Black, Puerto Rican, and Radical Studies courses, end to the tracking systems, cops, narcs, and security guards out of the schools! "We're making a revolution—join us!"

Police officers are referred to as "pigs." Demands are issued which essentially call for the administration to surrender its authority to control the students' activities. Presumably, these students want to choose their own courses, inevitably of the Marxist or anarchist variety, violate the drug laws on campus with sanction of the school authorities, and devote their class time to promoting a political revolution for the New Left. They also want permission to distribute these materials, urging other students to join in the fun.

On what basis are high school students, fortunate to have made average grades in a beginning United States history course, entitled to rewrite the curriculum, run the school, violate the laws, preach their obscenities and revolutionary schemes, *to the exclusion* of all other students who do not subscribe to their beliefs?

Yet efforts to limit this type of activity are predictable; the "progressives" talk about freedom of the press, and the poor student radicals who are being denied the "right," at the ripe old age of fifteen or sixteen to turn the high-school campus into a revolutionary cell.

The second example is the police department that announces a plan to search students' lockers without their permission. Immediately, we are reminded of a police state without the protection against search and seizure. The media, the interpreters, the open-minded progressives, join "the kids" in their idealistic protest against the grim, intimidating police villains.

Before you join the hue and cry about police brutality, consider the following:

A man signs in as a visitor to an elementary school during "Open School Week," then enters a classroom and robs the teacher.

A group of non-students enter a high-school campus and assault a school administrator.

Gang members are seen carrying sawed-off shotguns on campus.

A suspect is stopped by police on the steps of the high school; he is carrying an eight-inch kitchen knife.

A high-school student is arrested for carrying a .38 caliber revolver.

Five girls, including two high-school students, stripped and beat a fifteen-year-old girl from another high school.

A teenage boy shoves a ninety-year-old woman to the sidewalk during a purse snatching; she dies, he gets a dollar.

Sixty gun episodes take place in Los Angeles in a single school year.

Fifteen handguns are confiscated in Atlanta schools. A twelve-year-old boy, who disobeyed traffic signals, was angry at other students who laughed at him. He opened fire on the school ground.

Fifteen gun incidents occur in each of the following cities in a single school year: Detroit, New York, Kansas City.

The decision by the police to search the students' lockers is denounced by advocates of student rights; these civil libertarians are evidently not disturbed regarding another student right. This right belongs principally to those non-militants who do not issue non-negotiable demands: the right to attend school and go to class without being shot.

Arthur Miller, a distinguished playwright, publishes a statement asking if we can possibly doubt that all of our problems—war, poverty, discrimination, and every other misfortune—would disappear from the earth if everyone over thirty simply vanished. He also makes a plea for misguided adults to stop "turning against our children."

Often advocates of the youth cult are articulate, famous, and accomplished in the scholarly or artistic fields. Miller's assumption is that of "youthful innocence" and "mature corruption." He assumes that a society composed exclusively of the young would be idealistic, pure, and totally founded on moral principles. Miller forgets that the young, like everyone else, are people; the younger generation has its members who achieve the extremes of good and evil; most are somewhere in between.

Consider the following examples of "our children" at work and play:

The *New York Times* reports an increase of 174% in shoplifting. More than fifty percent are juveniles, especially suburban junior-high-school youngsters.

A school girl arrested for shoplifting describes her motive: "To prove I was groovy."

Another juvenile shoplifter describes a club in which the admission requirement is stealing, combined with successful lying to one's parents about the real source of the stolen goods.

Five hundred high-school students walk out of class, set fire to a basement, then run around the neighborhood, in the words of the student paper, "doing things."

A fire starts early in the morning, and a high school is evacuated. Four hundred students visit the principal to present their "non-negotiable" demands.

High-school students burn an American flag and go on a rampage throughout the school.

Arthur Miller should remember that Willy Loman, in *Death of a Salesman*, was destroyed partially by his lack of perception regarding himself and the world around him. Not all high-school students engage in the above activities. But these are the students who receive sympathetic attention in the press.

In recent months it has become fashionable to tag labels on to citizens. Of prime importance is one's classification. In the past, being an American meant just that. The man who emphasized age, sex, or race in making decisions was practicing discrimination. Now, however, labeling has become important. Like Arthur Miller, a large segment of the population assumes the sanctity and purity of ideas which ostensibly emanate from the younger generation. These well-meaning citizens are so busy being receptive to the young that they never stop to ask themselves what happens to the students who do *not* side with the militants, the young men and women who do not share the attitudes of the counterculture?

In the business world, youth has become a prime selling point. The maxim, never trust anyone over thirty, has been transformed, Madison Avenue style, into "Never hire anyone over thirty." The emphasis on youth has forced a continued cycle of dependence on the noisiest, most radical, least responsible segment of our youthful population. On close examination, the social analysts are trying to divide society into categories right out of a Hollywood B-Western. Those who do not favor an integration in society of those attitudes and behavioral practices of the youth cult are portrayed as villains, in favor of wars, repression, pollution, and perhaps even the common cold. The heroes are supposed to be young, creative, dynamic, and progressive.

In the coming pages, we shall examine some basic attitudes and elements of the counterculture of the 1960's, with their new relevance to controversies of the 1970's; we shall consider the culture of some young people which is offered mistakenly in the name of all young people. We shall see why many Americans find this new culture abhorrent, why it can be rejected by both young and old, and why its open-minded advocates have closed minds when dealing with this brand of criticism. Some of these elements will be theoretical, dealing with the whys and wherefores of radical politics; others will be cultural, concerned with music, films, literature, and fashions; still others will deal with medical questions (i.e., drugs) and morality.

Ultimately, we will recognize this new youth cult as an assault upon our traditional values. The youth cult cannot succeed without the abolition or radical alteration of most of our traditional institutions and attitudes toward the family, marriage, the work ethic, traditional artistic standards, taste, manners, republican form of government, and morality. The facts will speak for themselves. An examination of the youth cult will quickly reveal it to be hollow, hypocritical, and superficial. Instead, we will consider the alternatives.

The picture is not entirely bleak; just as Alice left the Mad Tea Party and returned to a world of rational beings, so can we still escape the political jungle and cultural vacuum offered by the youth cult. We shall see that the "old" values do work and are valid. If they have not created the perfect society, it is because man is imperfect. In our imperfection, we do not always behave according to our professed principles and ideals. Young America is by no means homogeneous in its taste or outlook. This is the view of a segment of young America that has been silenced because a benevolent élite of college professors, politicians, pseudo–intellectuals, and "thinkers" have chosen to ignore it.

The 1960's were years of harsh and destructive change for this country. The 1970's offer a challenge; we can recognize the counterculture and its intellectual offspring, the youth cult, as an aberration, and we can revitalize our institutions and principles, or we can watch our society fall apart. The choice is ours.

II.

Hiss the Villain:
The Politics of Paranoia

Like all fantasies and fairy tales, the youth-cult wonderland has a villain. This villain is omnipotent, rational, portrayed in such a way as to incur the wrath of any man, woman, or child who possesses even a grain of human feeling.

The villain is faceless, weightless, and formless, but certainly not nameless. Who is the villain held responsible for the ills of our nation? All the evidence points to one obvious source upon which we may place the blame for all of our problems. Some protestors have chosen to call it the "system," others the "corporate state," more often than not the villain is simply referred to as the Establishment.

Membership in the Establishment is loosely defined. Anyone may be accused of belonging to the Establishment if he or she happens to be on the opposite side of the political fence from his or her accuser. If you do not know whether or not you belong to the Establishment the chances are that you do. Denunciation of the Establishment has become an almost ritualistic requirement for advocates of the youth cult. Unlike the Boy Scouts, opponents of the Establishment do not help little, elderly ladies across the street.

The general assumption surrounding these denunciations of the Establishment is that the nation, unlike all Gaul, is divided into only two parts: them and us.

"Them" refers to all individuals and institutions with power or influence: the United States government, foundations, business

29

corporations, labor unions, university communities, etc. "Us" presumably represents the downtrodden minorities who have no influence or power.

The theory collapses faster than a house of cards. Far from the intimidating, repressive Establishment, society has shown a remarkable toleration of diverse points of view. The United States has survived because it is a free society; unfortunately, amid the blessings of the Bill of Rights and free speech, there are some undesirable influences. Absolute free speech does not include or justify the right to shout "fire" in a crowded theater. If men are free to speak, they may choose to abuse the privilege through lies, distortion, agitation, and the spreading of rumors. Traditionally, speech has been restricted in this country when it treads upon the rights of others. A man intent on committing libel or slander will find his self-styled "right" to engage in these acts subject to restriction. We do not take away free speech, because we cherish it more than we value the security of a society policed by Big Brother. But we should never forget that in the last decade, Americans have bent over backward in toleration of bizarre and radical political ideas; this has been the case even when these ideas have encouraged violence. In fact, as we shall shortly see, some citizens have been so open-minded to the politics of radicalism that they have maintained closed minds regarding everything else.

The politics of paranoia are founded on a neat assumption. The ills of the world are blamed on the Establishment; no specific solutions or programs are offered, but we are advised that all our problems would go away if the Establishment would just disappear. Occasionally the zeal for hastening the demise of the Establishment gets a little out of hand, as at the Columbia University rally in which the "students" shouted, "Kill all adults." These outbursts, however, are explained away by the press as manifestations of youthful enthusiasm.

In the 1960's, American society was dominated by controversies regarding the Vietnam War. The campus scenes of violence have been analyzed in depth elsewhere; there is no need to revive the whole question here. But an end, at least on paper, to the military battles in Vietnam, has not eclipsed a large and highly significant issue. At the height of the Vietnam controversy, some Americans claimed for themselves a "right" to stop American society in its tracks. They declared that the United States government should not function because they disagreed with its policies. They demanded that giant universities bow to their will and close down or restructure their classes in order that a specific ideological element on the campus be given control of the school's destiny.

Ultimately, these events led to a startling phenomenon: the New Politics, and more specifically, the New Left. Essential to both these movements was the self-proclaimed right of a revolutionary movement in the United States to impose a revolution on the rest of society. The question becomes not the pros and cons of the Vietnam War, but rather, the politics of paranoia. In the New Politics, any act can be justified as a reaction to the repression, real or imaginary, of the Establishment.

In the 1970's, the campuses have quieted down. Many young Americans have decided to work within the system rather than attempting to overthrow it. The change has been subtle, but significant. The rock-throwing campus radical has disappeared; very possibly, he has joined the faculty.

We may seem relieved that some students have abandoned violent change in favor of peaceful change. But peaceful change in the wrong direction is still small consolation to those who want to see our society progress and evolve. Many Americans are inclined to forget that only "mad" guests have been welcome at America's Mad Tea Party. Young people who feel ill at ease in the New Politics are not invited to attend.

Let us see some examples of the New Politics at work. In each of these examples, we shall find that the rhetoric of the New Left and its actions are consistently inconsistent.

All power to the people (of the afternoon kindergarten class). In the New Politics, it has become fashionable for a group of dissenters to declare themselves spokesmen for "the people," and to issue a set of demands. These demands may be directed against businessmen or against an administrator of a university. Often, the unfortunate victim of these demands is so eager to please the "people's representatives," that he never has time to find out whether these "representatives" were ever chosen to represent anyone.

For instance, political rallies at the Berkeley campus of the University of California often included persons described in the press as "non-students" or "street people." The latter were, not surprisingly, people who wandered on to the campus from the street. They liked the surroundings and decided that they should be given power to run the school and its curriculum their own way. At one point, campus radicals would transport students from San Francisco State to Berkeley and Berkeley radicals to San Francisco State. Some militants made a career of visiting one campus after another around the country, stirring up demonstrations as "non-students."

The long, bitter strike at San Francisco State was affected to a large degree by the strikers' "non-negotiable" demands. This declaration itself indicated that the strikers were not interested in negotiating or in discussion, but only in taking charge of the campus. Students who did not wish to participate in the San Francisco or Berkeley radicals' activities were physically assaulted. Presumably these assaults were justified because they were instigated by the self-appointed "people's representatives," obviously to protect the students who were being beaten because they tried to attend class.

In the politics of paranoia, radicals demand that they be permitted to inflict their will on society. If society balks, they assume that it is society's fault. For instance, we are told that high schools do not function as democracies. Presumably, they do not allow for "student objectivity." One function of a school is the responsibility to guide, teach, and develop. Should teachers approach moral questions on the grounds that "all sides" merit a hearing, both the moral and immoral? Should an English teacher assume that two viewpoints, the literate and illiterate, deserve to be considered with equal attention? The teacher who objects to such youthful utterances as "where it's at," "like it is," "uptight," "grooving along," "stoned," and various unprintables thus becomes a repressor.

Extending this principle further, we might experiment with discussion of the "legal" and "illegal" alternatives available to students. The former could be presented by judges and lawyers, while the latter would be equally represented by various felons, terrorists, and perhaps a mugger from Central Park. Both views, of course, would have to be monitored by the teacher without showing any favoritism.

A school, like a family, is not a democracy. It is a highly specialized unit that performs highly specialized functions. Should students be permitted to use obscenities to their teachers? Is filthy speech a "student right?" Should fourth-graders be allowed to smoke marijuana or tobacco?

One of the functions of a school is the establishment of rules and regulations that encourage an environment that is conducive to learning. If the school abdicates its responsibilities, it abandons its primary function. Freedom and license are not synonymous. A public interest *does* exist and its protection is the responsibility and duty of the public sector of our society.

What we have observed about the school is equally applicable to the society in general. Companies that issue standards for dress or behavior are accused of perpetuating a corporate state monopoly. Consider the case of a man who engages in a public service by managing a small shop. Let us speculate on the dilemma that is raised if the man hires someone to work for him. The shop owner may be selling groceries. If his employee chooses to wait on customers while standing on his head, and customers do not find this posture reassuring, what should be done? Should the shopkeeper be compelled to lose his customers in deference to the young man's eccentricity? If the young man wants to wear dirty clothing in the grocery store and track unsanitary filth around the food, does he have a right to do this? Who should decide? A "people's committee"? Robots? Computers? Yippies? Academicians?

If the young man wants to wear a barrel and walk upside-down, he has a right to do so, but not when these rights infringe upon the equally respectable rights and privileges of others. Employees have no special right to force their employers to respond to their whims. Students have no right to run a school. This does not imply that workers do not have rights of collective bargaining; but when stage personnel play cards backstage and fill out their union quotas while a Broadway production goes on without them, because the production required one stagehand, the practice is carried too far.

When a segment of ill-educated students insists that a university bow to its non-negotiable demands to offer courses in riot and rebellion, events have gone too far.

Much of today's New Left rhetoric deals with the Revolution. Vague comparisons are made between the Berrigan brothers and the Adams brothers, between Jane Fonda and Thomas Paine. At the time of the American Revolution, the colonists did not receive legitimate redress of grievances.

Read the Declaration of Independence carefully. Jefferson made clear the legitimate grievances the colonists had against the English Crown. But the cry was "Taxation without representation." The New Left is unhappy not because they are without representation, but because they were not chosen as our representatives.

Next on the agenda may be a discussion of the rights of kindergarten students to abolish arithmetic and reading. Doesn't every school child have a right to issue non-negotiable demands to devote his life to recess?

Thomas Carlyle once declared, "I do not believe in the collective wisdom of individual ignorance." He had the answer.

The egalitarian ideal: all men are created equal, but those under thirty are more equal than those over thirty. This slight alteration of the Jeffersonian ideal seems to have permeated the New Politics. In 1972, unlike 1968, young people were much a participatory part of the election process. The voting age was lowered; presumably this was the invitation to "our children" to join the electoral process. Political prognosticators predicted the inevitability of the leftward swing of America's youth. One prediction declared, "If half the newly eligible youths vote, and two-thirds vote Democratic, Nixon could lose nine states he won in 1968."

Clearly, these predictions did not possess their validity. The McGovern campaign was ultimately one of the least successful in our history. Yet the Miami Democratic Convention was represented to the public as an exercise in pure democracy. We were told that the political professionals were ousted, and that "real Americans" were taking over the mainstream of society and politics. Certainly, the demonstrators who picketed the convention hall in Chicago in 1968 were inside the hall in Miami in 1972.

Imposed on the convention, however, was a quota system, a means of labeling delegates by the racial or sexual classification. Each state had to have a specific number of men and women, a specific percentage of racial representation. These quotas are offered as a justification for the new egalitarian claims of the New Politics. The difficulty is that the McGovern Democrats chose their quotas on the basis of several selected and favorable minority groups: blacks, Chicanos, and Indians. They chose men and women. They ignored the Chinese, Irish, Italians, Poles, etc. There is no specific basis for determining these quotas. Traditionally, Americans have been Americans, pure and simple, not hyphenated Americans, with an ethnic, racial, or sexual qualification. To carry this quota scheme to its logical extreme, every possible minority group would have to be given its percentage. Non-ethnic minorities (i.e., midgets, for instance) would have to be given their percentage. Myopic individuals could rally against the denial of the nearsighted quota. Basketball players had an obvious complaint. How many delegates were seven feet tall? Left-handed citizens were not polled to discover whether the delegations had been established through practices which discriminated against southpaws. In fact, the rationale of the quota systems is obviously practical. Those groups who were favorable to the youth cult and its political manifestation, McGovernism, were supported for large quotas. Those who were not favorable, by and large, to McGovernism were not supported for large quotas.

Ultimately, this form of electioneering can be refined and developed. A candidate favored by a large segment of professional wrestlers or amateur jugglers can insist on their quotas, to the exclusion of those groups which are unfavorable to his views (i.e., circus clowns and college professors). This criticism of the quota scheme does not imply that black, Chicano, and Indian citizens are not entitled to their representation at conventions. But rather, we must recognize that making racial or religious characteristics a condition of employment is unwise.

The quotas of young people at the Democratic Convention were allegedly an example of democracy at work. But by what right do we assume that inexperienced young people are necessarily entitled to the same degree of representation at a political convention as their elders, based totally on their percentage in the population?

The convention's young people were presented to the general public as "representatives of our children." Yet when the final votes were counted, observers were surprised that a large segment of the youthful populace had voted for Richard Nixon. They had assumed that the nation was divided along percentage lines of taste similar to the percentages of the convention quotas. Among non-college youth, Richard Nixon and George McGovern did as well as they did with voters of other ages. Even the campus vote, presumably oriented toward the New Politics, was considerably less favorable to the New Left programs which had been introduced in the Democratic caucuses.

In recent months, the quota scheme has been used in universities. A *National Review* editorial reports, "The quota system already is in semiclandestine operation in college admissions and in the hiring of faculty, and gallows-wit jokes are circulating in the faculty lounges. ('She couldn't get a job in Anthropology as an Eskimo. She's trying English as a lesbian.')"

Superficially, the New Politics favors a democratic procedure. But to arbitrarily divide the nation into quotas and percentages and to represent this process as "democracy at work" is a sham. The ethnic or theological gerrymander is an old political trick; but with the New Politics, it is cloaked in the mantle of social reform.

The best of both possible worlds. The political paranoids discovered quickly that being anti-Establishment was chic and fashionable. They learned that society tends to sympathize with Bob Cratchit, but jeers at Ebeneezer Scrooge. The solution was clear: advocates of the New Politics would play the old politics, but drape themselves in the mantle of a downtrodden minority. (Enough minority groups have legitimate grievances as to make open-minded citizens hesitant to see through this charade. Thus, the radicals became darlings of the social élite, often rich and famous, and all the while, achieving the notoriety by denouncing the Establishment.)

In truth, the real Establishment is the élite assembly of pseudo-intellectuals who pride themselves on understanding the younger generation. The news media and publishing industries have been especially guilty in this respect. By assuming the sanctity of New Politics ideals, they have created a false set of ambitious idols who have spuriously claimed to represent the interests of the poor and downtrodden.

Consider for instance, the obvious example of the self-styled radicals, Abbie Hoffman and Jerry Rubin. Superficially, Hoffman and Rubin are trying to overthrow the Establishment. It is hard to understand why because they have discovered successful careers as professional revolutionaries. Hoffman and Rubin are deeply involved in royalty checks, sales percentages, lecture fees, book and film contracts, and the world of literary agents.

Christopher Cerf, a Random House editor who worked with Hoffman, remarked, "He talks about advances. He talks about percentages of things. He knows what he's doing. His lawyer and business agent, Jerry Lefcourt, says, "He'd probably be worth $250,000 on Madison Avenue." Rubin's attitude on law and order is also curious. He says, "When planning a demonstration, always include a role for the cops. Most people don't get excited until the cops come in. Nothing radicalizes like a cop. Cops are perfectly dressed for the role of the bad guy."

Rubin's book, which he publicized at every opportunity, was entitled *Do It!* The reader was encouraged to do anything, so long as it caused society to fall apart. Rubin commented, "The goal of the book is to destroy the system . . . it's a Molotov cocktail. The whole purpose of the book is to spread chaos." Rubin does not like policemen, but he loves the copyright office, especially for protecting his rights. Hoffman's two books earned more than $50,000 in advances, royalties, and resale rights; he expected $25,000 in additional funds as a percentage of a motion picture sale. Hoffman and Rubin are uncomplicated; they like money, power, and fame; if they can fill their bank accounts while tearing up society in general, they will be quick to do so.

But what of Christopher Cerf at Random House? What of Hillard Elkins, who expressed enthusiastic interest in a film based on Hoffman's writings? Elkins, whose production of the all-nude

Oh Calcutta! earned him no reputation for artistic profundity, is nonetheless a successful film and stage producer. It is difficult to understand why these men would want to see the system torn down, especially since they have profited so well from it. Hoffman is starring in a movie which will feature his own vasectomy, and writing his sexual autobiography, *Kiss and Tell.* Yet one of the nation's most prestigious lecture bureaus told the author, "Of course we'd handle Hoffman or Rubin. If we can keep them out of jail, they're sensational. If we didn't make money out of them, someone else would!"

This is the double standard! This is hypocrisy. While the publishers and newsmen are following the Hoffmans and Rubins around, hanging on their every word, responsible youth are hard-pressed to obtain even a hearing. To the contrary, they ridicule the young men and women who are responsible. Lucian K. Truscott IV, writing in *Saturday Review* about the young voters who favored the President, said, "These weren't the kids that I see on Greenwich Village streets, on their way to classes at NYU. They looked too . . . clean cut and fresh, that is. The girls had the well-scrubbed look that comes with just the right amount of makeup, almost a virginal aura. And the guys all looked like student-council presidents at their local high schools, the kind who get their names in the local paper before they're fifteen."

The Nixon family was characterized as "dressed for a high-school prom," and their family loyalty was discussed with the implied suspicion that it was too good to be true. The news media, watching the Convention like a gloom squad, frowned and fretted about the contrivance of the neatly scrubbed Establishment young people. Obviously, these student-body president types shouting, "Four more years" were not really representative of "our brightest intellectual minds."

In portraying the New Left as an anti-Establishment minority, the news media have compounded their errors. They have made it easy, even inviting, for young men and women to gain notoriety by espousing an assortment of radical causes. Often this is accomplished not by direct lies, but by distortions and characterization. Readers and television viewers become justifiably confused because the middle man—the journalist—presents the facts in such a way as to create a totally false impression of what has actually taken place.

In Berkeley, proponents of leash laws were denounced as "anti-dog"; publicity campaigns suggested that the anti-canine villains were trying to destroy man's best friend. Newspapers ran pictures of lovable little puppies; the issue, however, was not the helpless puppy, but the aimless, intimidating, and sometimes vicious pack of stray dogs that found Berkeley a haven for their more primitive canine instincts.

Incidents like the Berkeley leash laws may seem unimportant; but when similar distortions are applied to controversies of national significance, the question of journalistic responsibility is quickly brought into question.

For instance, the communications men will characterize the "protest of America's leading theologians against the horrors of war and the Establishment." The gullible reader may conclude that if these views are respectable enough for the Roman Catholic church, they may be valid for him as well. When the Reverend Daniel Berrigan, S.J. draws comparisons between Jesus Christ and Ché Guevara, the Cuban Communist revolutionary, his credibility as both theologian and political analyst are in doubt. Discussions about the Students for a Democratic Society and their radical Weathermen faction seldom focused on the true nature of their political protests. A declaration signed by Bernadine Dohrn and the Weathermen reflected this organization's peaceful intentions: "Two weeks before the townhouse explosion, four members of this group had firebombed Judge Murtagh's house in New York as an action of support for the Panther Twenty-one, whose trial was just beginning. To many people this was a very good action. Within the group, however, the feeling developed that because this action had not done anything to hurt the pigs materially, it wasn't very important. So within two weeks time, this group had moved from firebombing to anti-personnel bombs. Many people in the collective did not want to be involved in the large-scale, almost random bombing offensive that was planned. But they struggled day and night and eventually, everyone agreed to do their part." But the declaration went on to state, "People become revolutionaries in the schools, in the army, in prisons, in communes, and on the streets. Not in an underground cell."

The literary agent, Alex Jackinson, encountered one of the New Left writers, James Simon Kunen, shortly after the publication of Kunen's book, *The Strawberry Statement*. Kunen appeared at a writers' conference wearing what Jackinson called regulation rebels' garb: old jeans with shirttails hanging out. Jackinson went on to remark, "Most of those who prate peace in Vietnam do not really want peace; they want a Vietcong victory. At least an American military defeat." Jackinson characterized the new "revolution" as "fragmentation, withdrawal into desperation, individual acts of terror, into communes, into drugs, rock, and sex."

Jackinson's observations were well taken. At the end of the Vietnam War, the nation seemed more quiet, ready to pause for a moment in hope that the peace would last. The hard-core radicals will continue to agitate, but many of those persons who are only sympathetic to the New Politics will be rejoining society to work within the system. Certainly the hippies are gone as a major influence, a historical social phenomenon that disappeared into the shadows of our recent past. But in these rapidly changing times, the critics and self-styled intellectuals will not let the counter-culture die of its own accord. Instead, they want to urge society in general to adopt the various social and political perspectives which permeated the counterculture of the 1960's.

The intellectuals' embrace of the counterculture was predictable and lost no time in coming. A Yale Professor of Law, Charles Reich, wrote a book called *The Greening of America*. Reich's book, which immediately became a bestseller, was hailed by such stalwart liberals as George McGovern and William O. Douglas. Schoolteachers, parents, and well-meaning adults of all ages wrote to Reich thanking him for explaining that the kids were really all right after all.

Reich's thesis essentially was that conservatives were trying to turn the clock back in opposition to change, that liberals were busy trying to change the world through institutions, and that only the young people would be successful because they would start a peaceful, non-violent cultural revolution. This revolution, we were told, would come about only through individual conversion rather than through violent change. Reich then proceeded to write a long apologia for the youth cult, slobbism, rock music, and the drug culture. He assigned impressive labels to the conservatives (Consciousness I), liberals (Consciousness II), and revolutionaries, peaceful or otherwise (Consciousness III). But Reich's ideal social unit turned out to be the commune, his celebration of life, the rock festival, his model form of municipal cooperation, the co-op supermarket at Berkeley. The rock festival is approximately as peaceful in a tranquil community as a herd of stampeding elephants downtown at rush hour. The squalor, filth, and blatant immorality of the Berkeley radicals does not speak well for Consciousness III. Although Reich tried to give the revolution respectability, his arguments were devoid of logic, and ultimately, instead of raising the level of the dropout culture, he inadvertently exposed its weaknesses, as well as those of some of the faculty members of our universities.

For a while, hippies (or hustling writers who dressed like hippies) became the fashionable guests at literary parties. Today, with the collapse of the McGovern campaign, the Reich theories seem to have evaporated. But the real danger is that the manners and tastes and political indiscretions of the counterculture, a grim failure, will be absorbed into the mainstream of the national culture. Recently, the radical Yippie leaders were honored guests as lecturers in a major university. Alice Cooper, the male rock-group leader who includes his own simulated hanging as part of his act, was invited to appear at the Eastman School of Music as lecturer. High-school students clamor to hear the latest denunciation of our national goals by Jane Fonda.

By and large, the violent revolution of the 1960's failed. With the end of the war, many of those sympathetic to that revolt will be tempted to rethink their positions. But if the illogical, immature, but potentially vicious nature of the counterculture politics was a disaster outside the mainstream, it will be doubly so if it ever becomes respectable.

A recent poll indicated that Americans admire doctors; the group that they admired next to last was politicians, next to used-car salesmen. The counterculture had no program; it has none now that it has become respectable. The campus radical had nothing constructive to offer in the 1960's; he has little more to contribute now, even if he is engaged in writing his doctoral dissertation on the demise of the Establishment. The bad taste and overt vulgarity of the dropouts will add nothing worthwhile to American society simply because their proponents have dropped back in again and are running for public office instead of throwing things at the politicians they dislike.

The New Politics, when examined, is too much like the old politics: it offers peace, prosperity, brotherhood, and something for nothing. It stands behind the claims 1000%!

III.
"Rock" Is a Four-Letter Word!

If any single medium of expression could be said to represent the youth culture in the mind of the general public, it is "rock," a term established through truncated use of "rock and roll," the popular teenage dance music that has suddenly assumed a role of social significance in our daily lives.

It is impossible to escape rock, should one desire to do so. It is on television, on radio, on record. Rock groups may be heard at the most élite parties of the wealthy and socially prominent who are described as "beautiful people"; they also may be heard at your local high-school basketball game.

What is this phenomenon, described by one observer as a "protean music capable of almost limitless expression?" On the surface, at least, eminently respectable! Leaders of rock groups are rich and famous. The most famous group, the Beatles, was decorated by the Queen of England. A national organization of music teachers has advocated introducing rock in the school system, and one of the most bizarre group leaders has been invited to lecture at an old and widely regarded university. Rock groups have appeared in concert with symphony orchestras, to the delight of such conductors as Leonard Bernstein and Zubin Mehta, and have been welcomed into the homes and parties of the status-conscious literary circles, with the full approval of the latter's social arbiter, Truman Capote. Rock music is criticized with a reverence formerly reserved only for the nation's most distinguished concert music. All in all, rock music seems respectable.

In a day and age when it is fashionable to ridicule the flag, and motherhood is subject to the daily tirades of women's liberationists, rock music has become something of a sacred cow. The critical observer who reaches for his earplugs when the electric guitars are plugged in and the amplifiers are turned up is asking for trouble.

But we have already dared to rush in where angels and music critics alike fear to tread and will soon discover some surprising truths about the rock-music phenomenon. Some of these truths relate to music, some to morals, and all to money. Ultimately, they will reveal the massive fraud that has been perpetrated upon society, aided and abetted by those citizens whose fear of being called "old-fashioned" has caused them to check their common sense (and their eardrums) at the nearest rock-concert ticket window.

From the beginning, rock music has grown through the interaction of two elements: teenage rebellion and fast-talking promoters. The managers responsible for creating the rock phenomenon are not unlike used-car salesmen. Success or failure is measured as much by the manager as by the performers themselves. The Beatles, four young Englishmen in their twenties, living in Liverpool, began an early phase of their careers under the management of an over-thirty nightclub owner, Allan Williams. "I couldn't have done what Brian Epstein did for them," admitted Williams, "nor what he did for Gerry and the Pacemakers." In a reference to Brian Epstein, Williams was acknowledging what most middle-aged apologists for rock refuse to recognize as even in existence: the commercial fraternity of rock promoter-managers who are personally responsible for the billion dollar industry with all its ramifications. For Brian Epstein, like Colonel Tom Parker before him, was responsible for managing and manipulating the careers of pop-music idols. What has this to do with the "profound philosophical revolution" associated with the counterculture? Nothing, and this is precisely the point. A brief examination of the history of rock (as seen by those familiar with the London, New York, Hollywood, and Nashville recording industries) reveals that the initial origins of rock were anything but sociological. Bill Haley was one of the first rock stars, and some teenagers who saw his film, *Rock Around the Clock*, when it was released in 1956, responded by tearing up the theater. The event was, in some ways, prophetic. Although proponents of rock music preach "peace" in their public relations communications, the phenomenon has always been associated with the frustrations of teenagers. In the 1950's, this rebellion was turned against forms of authority: parents, school, and restrictions of any kind. But in the 1960's, combined with the drug culture and egged on by violent political revolutionaries, the rebellion took an even uglier turn. Haley was soon eclipsed by another star, a young man named Elvis Presley.

Elvis Presley, generally considered to be the first superstar of the rock world, began his career around the Nashville radio stations. Dewey Phillips, a former disc jockey, recalls the early Presley: "Nobody was picking upon the ole boy back then. He was a real bashful kid, but he liked to hang around music. They'd chased him away from the switchboard at WMPS, and he'd come hang around Q. That's WHBG, where I was doing my show, 'Red Hot and Blue,' every night. Weekends, he'd come down to Sun Records—he'd cut that record, 'My Happiness' for his mother, paid four dollars for it himself, and Sam Phillips, president of Sun, finally gave him a session. He tried to record a ballad, *but he couldn't cut it.*"

Is this the Elvis Presley whose brash confidence worried the mothers of teenage daughters during the 1950's? Curiously enough, Presley still considered himself a country-western singer during this period, when he tried to follow Phillips' advice on his first radio interview, "Just don't say nothing dirty." Presley's rock career improved, however, when he came under the guidance of the incredible Colonel Tom Parker. Who was Parker? Stanley Booth, writing in *Esquire*, provides the answer: "Thomas Andrew Parker, a latter-day Barnum out of W. C. Fields by William Burroughs. A carnival orphan, he had worked in his uncle's 'Great Parker Pony Circus,' dipped candied apples, shaved ice for snow cones, operated merry-go-rounds, even put in a stretch as a dog catcher in Tampa, Florida." But Parker was not a man to be held down by the fortunes of life. Soon Presley was appearing on the "Ed Sullivan Show," earning $50,000 for three appearances. When Presley returned home, Parker arranged for him to appear at a charity benefit. After three hours of waiting for other performers to finish their acts, the audience finally got to see Presley, who

proceeded, according to Stanley Booth, to simulate sexual intercourse with the microphone.

It is significant that public attention was focused exclusively on
the now-venerated Presley. "The Colonel" has avoided the
limelight. If one refers to "The Colonel" today, most Americans
are more likely to think of the manufacturer of prepackaged
fried-chicken dinners than a star-maker out of P. T. Barnum.

If Presley's gyrations upset the mothers of America, off stage
and off camera he was reputed to behave like a gentleman. He
addressed his employers in the recording industry as "Sir," or
"Ma'am." Presley thus offset his onstage antics with an ingenuous
private image. If this made his performance more respectable,
some observers were not fooled. Unlike the singing idols of the
1940's, particularly Frank Sinatra, Presley did not sing about
romance or mooonlight or sing the poetic lyrics of Oscar Hammer-
stein. According to rock historian Nik Cohn, the teenage girls who
screamed at Presley's concerts had no time for sighing, swooning,
and sobbing. He recalls, "With rock though, it's all been down to
mainline sexual fantasy. Sitting in concert halls, school girls have
screamed, rioted, brawled, and fainted. They've wet themselves
and they've masturbated. According to P. J. Proby, they've even
ripped the legs off their chairs and mauled themselves. They've
done all kinds of outrageous stuff they'd never do anywhere else,
and they've been so uninhibited because there has always been a
safety belt, because the pop singer himself has been unreachable,
unreal, and nothing could actually happen." Nor had the situation
changed by the late 1960's, when Cohn reportedly became bored
with the viciousness of the Rolling Stones after a concert and
returned to the deserted auditorium. He reported again that "the
small girls had screamed too hard and wet themselves. Not just one
or two of them, but many, so that the floor was sodden and the
stench was overwhelming."

The use of a rock concert as a sexual stimulant was the
beginning; the end was the Roman orgy, contemporary style, with
bell-bottoms replacing togas, and packaged under the label of
Woodstock. The mothers who feared for their daughters' morality
in the 1950's were not unjustified. A recent article by Sam
Sutherland, writing in *Penthouse*, declares, "In the early 1970's, it

has come to pass that rock 'n' roll appears to have revealed itself as precisely what mom and dad feared it might be: sex."

The rock stars who followed Presley were of many varieties. Each had his own particular image, carefully molded by his manager, with clothing, life-style, and personality designed to follow the trends. Screamin' Jay Hawkins, whose career began back in the 1940's, emerged flaming from a coffin, carrying a smoking skull. Little Richard pounded the piano keyboard with the heel of his foot. Jerry Lee Lewis virtually attacked the piano with his feet and fists, and finally closed his act by jumping on top of the piano. The trends changed. Rock songs began emphasizing the youth culture that existed in high school. Political revolutionaries hadn't yet gained an influence on the high-school campus, and life seemed to be a continuous array of dates, cokes, hamburgers, french fries, parties, and music. The boys wore crew cuts, the girls pony-tails. Parents were "square," but they'd come around, eventually. Rock songs talked about lipstick, love, dating, being sweet sixteen, girl friends, and boy friends. The trends changed again. The record promoters tried the "Twist," a dancing fad from the Peppermint Lounge in New York, which became fashionable. This time, not only the teenagers but the rich and famous middle-aged adults tried "twisting." Chubby Checker, a former chicken plucker from Philadelphia, recorded the tune, "Let's Twist Again," a revival of an old rock song. Checker became the subject of a variety of promotions ranging from the Chubby Checker T-shirts to Chubby Checker dolls. The twist was eventually replaced by a variety of dances, all performed alone; none of the dances were related to the partnership of a couple dancing (or romancing) together. The dances changed, the names changed, and somehow remained the same: loud, noisy, and full of sexual display. The Beach Boys sang about surfing and hotrods, and both activities seemed preferable to homework in the minds of teenage boys.

The ultimate pop explosion came in the mid-1960's, in England, with the advent of the Beatles. Their rise has been chronicled in every possible medium, but little attention has been focused on the machinations of their manager, Brian Epstein. In the early days of their career, the Beatles were tough, greasy, lower-class pop musicians with few artistic pretensions. By the time Epstein had finished, they were undoubtedly the four most well-known young men in the world and for the millions of pounds they brought into England, the Queen gave them the M.B.E.

The Beatles, formerly an unsuccessful skiffle band in Liverpool, discovered their amplified sound in Germany, where, out of money, they could only afford two amplifiers for their four guitars. Paul McCartney declared, "We didn't worry about arrangements or anything. If we had trouble with our overworked amplifiers— we had to plug two guitars into one—I'd just chuck everything in and start leaping around the stage or rush to the piano and start playing some chords . . . it was noise and beat all the way."

Epstein, a twenty-six-year-old Englishman, set out to manage the Beatles as Parker had managed Elvis Presley. Far from being the unique, spontaneous art form which resulted from a ground-swell of sympathy and creative energy in the soul of America (or England), rock was initially and always a stylistic commodity which proved unsuccessful until managed by ambitious business-men. Some of the managers were as bizarre as the acts they promoted. Nik Cohn described the typical agent or record producer in these terms: "He hated pop but liked money. He was also often homosexual, and since his job lay mostly in discovering pretty young boys, this helped. He found the act he wanted and made a record. This record was then released, and either it sold or it was hyped." Columbia Records reportedly invested $200,000 in promotional fees to exploit the group which called itself The Moby Grape. The music industry was inundated by teenage tycoons in the 1960's, ranging from the mercurial record producer Phil Spector to the film industry's premiere entrepreneur, Mike Curb.

Curb, who presently functions as a Vice President of Metro-Goldwyn-Mayer, seems to be at variance with the idyllic descrip-tion of the rock artist as desiring "freedom from work." Have these "rock-tycoons" adopted the philosophy which their admirers applaud, Chet Powers' suggestion, "Smile on your brother/Every-body get together/Try to love one another right now?"

Journalist Sally Kempton, after being refused an interview by the elusive Albert Grossman, manager of Bob Dylan, recalled, "When it comes to the put-off, hip, New Style, today's sound producers and managers are virtually unsurpassed." She subsequently interviewed another leading manager, Phil Steinberg, whom she describes as "impeccably dressed in a shiny gray suit," in his green velvet office. When she arrived on schedule to interview an A and R man (Artists and Repertoire), she was informed by his secretary that he had not scheduled the appointment and had gone elsewhere. One of the most successful of all rock promoters, who prefers to remain anonymous, admitted to the author "I've made stars of untalented people; I did it for the money." Another of these manager-tycoons maintains an office on the Sunset Strip which is decorated entirely in expensive antiques.

Apologists for rock may feel that the method whereby their music achieved public attention is irrelevant if the quality of their work is good. (We shall deal with the quality of their work and their highly publicized life-style in a moment.) But to maintain that the pop-music idols are anything other than masterful creations of Madison Avenue geniuses, is to mislead the public into regarding rock as a form of musical populism, a spontaneous outgrowth of our national conscience. Eventually, rock lyricists turned to the political attitudes that permeated the high-school and college campuses, which will be discussed in a later chapter. But while the "rock experience" still has been a public exercise in sexual stimulation, critics seem to be intent on forgetting that the origin of our "national conscience" was once the musical medium of expression for the surfers celebrating the Banzai Pipeline and the philosophical or epistomological maturity of writhing teenagers on "American Bandstand," encouraged by an eager Dick Clark. (Clark, if your 1950's nostalgia escapes you, was the youthful master of ceremonies whose clean-cut appearance served to soften the blow for parents worried about their teenagers' idolatry of performers who were, by 1950's standards, "strange.") Clark was never convicted of accepting payola, but through Congressional hearings, he was revealed to be far more than the boy next door. A thoroughly capable entrepreneur, he was subsequently forced by ABC to divest himself of enterprises which the broadcasting company regarded as conflicting interests.)

The rock movement did not begin simultaneously with the influx of political radicalism on the campuses. The pop-record industry, absorbing an interest in surfing or beach parties or whatever happened to be the latest teenage fad, was equally ready to espouse political radicalism if the latter proved profitable.

The true nature of the record industry may be seen by those who ignore the superficial aura of glamor which seems to surround persons employed in the entertainment fields. Paul Ackerman, editor of *Billboard* (the bible of the record industry, because it enables record executives to see who has earned the most money), testified in Congressional hearings that payola (bribes used by record executives or their representatives to monopolize broadcast time with emphasis on "plugging" selected recordings) was standard procedure in the recording industry.

Recently, former Capitol Records executive, Roger Karshner, shocked the public with a new book, *The Music Machine*, in which he told about the record industry. Karshner describes an incredible world of phonies, phony billings, phony charts, phony trends, and mediocrity, stimulated by "payola, layola, flyola," and other forms of bribery and chicanery. He indicates that mass prostitution is a common inducement used at recording industry sales conventions, and recounts numerous incidents of stardom for untalented "musicians" who became overnight "superstars" and "country-western" performers who have seen neither the country nor the West. He also discusses "untalented megalomaniacs" who dominate the industry who speak only of "dynamic success," "dynamic sales," and "dynamic superstars," while those truly endowed with talent or abilities are often sent begging. A pop musician whose managerial backers are able to find a successful promotional technique for their client may suddenly be recognized as a "creative genius."

While musicians of a variety of tastes and levels are suffering nervous collapse en masse, for fear that someone will render them "obsolete" for failing to recognize the validity of "rock," the publicity machines continue to function.

Karshner comments, "Now the musical 'meat packers' go to work. The local sales organization orders voluminous quantities of the record to 'cover' the market in anticipation of consumer demands created by jingle-jangle radio. The record is shipped to every dealer, every rack jobber, and every one-stop. Stacks and racks of the record loom like black smokestacks on retail counters all over the city. The company is ready, prepared, armed; every salesman becomes a veritable wholesale minuteman prepared to die for absurdity." Karshner has courageously revealed what others refuse to admit, except in private.

As for the "social motivation" of "superstars," Karshner describes a typical example: a rich and influential young man who moves into an East Village apartment discovers the "social injustice" of being poor, and emerges as a protest singer. As the young man is promoted and publicized, he becomes a "superstar" who identifies with the oppressed and exploited. Ultimately, he identifies so much with these people that he learns to "hate" his country estate, his new Rolls Royce, his private airplane, his new home overlooking the ocean, and all the material possessions he regularly acquired. Most of all, he "hated" the millions of dollars he continued to earn, and of course, he "hated" society, businessmen, the government, the police, and everyone else.

Karshner also succeeded in recognizing much of the hypocrisy present in the recording industry. He decided to tell the truth about the new image which many of today's current record producers seek to project. He says, "There are many young people in publishing also. They're regaled in the latest garb of hippydom, peeking from behind scruffy hair with cool eyes. They look right, talk softly, and hasten to tell you that their "heads are together" and that their aim is on the creative target of free artistic expression. But underneath the Mickey Mouse T-shirts and behind the patches on the old Levis lies lurking little bald, overdressed, bent-over greedy-fingered midgets with cigar stained Masonic rings . . . and the markets are flooded and consumers are besieged with the oversold, overmerchandised, overadvertised dregs that are the residue of the big lie. . . ."

Karshner is not alone in recognizing the hollow spirits of these individuals. Nik Cohn commented, "Where the way to break the bubblegum market is simply to shout, to be louder and flashier and more vulgar than the competition, the avant-garde has to be breached by stealth, by intellectual flattery, by the suggestion that only the very finest minds can understand the product offered. On that basis, though, the intelligentsia is possibly even more gullible than the kids." The noted poet Karl Shapiro remarked, "The wave of male and female hysterics with guitars and brotherhood lyrics turned into a mass industry on one hand and on the other, a generation of revoltés without goals." Finally, Ernest Hemingway, hardly an unsophisticated observer, summed up that whole matter. He said, "We are deluged with writers who can't write, actors who can't act, and singers who can't sing . . . and they are all making a million dollars a year."

These matters may be of no interest to those who prefer to dwell on the "aesthetics" of rock. But such critics should remember that not one single rock song or lyric has been recorded without achieving in some measure the approval of these recording executives, and that anyone cognizant of the penthouse offices of New York rock promoters (or the Sunset Strip–Beverly Hills counterparts) is aware that these men regard themselves in private as "image-builders" capable of making any idea (or philosophical attitude) or any star "commercial" by cranking up the wheels of their multibillion dollar publicity machines. Those who talk about the spontaneity of rock blithely ignore the fact that many rock groups are not signed to record contracts. This is not because they are less cognizant of the cohesive cultural revolution he desires to portray, but because the powers that be which dominate the promotion and management in this field have not decided that their efforts should be made in behalf of these particular groups. If well-educated men want to persuade themselves or the public that the rise of any specific movement in rock is the result of ideological or stylistic timeliness, it's fine with the promoters. What does a former rock idol say about himself now that his career is in a stage of development in which he can afford to be honest? Fabian Forte, once known as "The Fabulous Fabian," says, "I could carry a tune, but that's about all. The rest was just ballyhoo."

In an effort to provide these commercially established rock groups with philosophical trappings, journalists and critics have made intensive efforts to emphasize the aesthetic progress made by the rock musicians in terms of creative endeavor. Significantly, they ignore the aesthetics of the rock groups who established their reputation through the beach-party films produced by the Holly-wood film factories. It is difficult, we must concede, to read social significance into a screen romance between Frankie Avalon and Annette Funicello.

We may distinguish between the trappings of the rock industry and the music and lyrics themselves. One of the more curious aspects of the entire pop-music situation is that those persons who do object to rock have concentrated almost totally upon the morality or political ideas of the performers. Few comments are made about the general level of musicianship. It is generally regarded as irreverent to speak of rock superstars as inept musicians who neither sing nor play particularly well. Their performances are characterized, more often than not, by references to "feeling" and "emotion," to that indescribable charisma which affects an audience when a true superstar walks out on the stage.

Public relations men have been hard pressed to find new terminology by which to describe their clients. But the pop-music industry has never suffered from a lack of creative imagination on the part of the advertising men, and true to form, they did not let their public down. The "new music" was born with a whole new set of standards to replace good voices or technical virtuosity in its evaluation. The result is a curious brand of "newspeak" worthy of George Orwell.

First, we are reminded that the rock groups exude "boundless energy." The music is amplified electronically, sometimes to such a decibel level that the words cannot be understood and the music becomes a deafening drone. This becomes rock's "complex texture." Rock groups are characterized as small cells of universal brotherhood in which young people participate, like Renaissance men, as composers. One inevitable bond between the rock group or soloist and the audience is that both presumably have taken drugs as an integral part of the musical experience. The groups live or work together in a commune, expressing their own "unique personalities." If they worked at any point in their careers in a discotheque, their performances are characterized as "multimedia experiences." The various media involved presumably include sex and drugs as well as the music. Finally, the lyrics are presented as a manifestation of poetry, a poignant effort to be heard amid the chaos and confusion that dominates the rest of the world.

This assortment of elements is expected to combine in an ocean of togetherness that is idyllic, tranquil, and disturbed only by the hostility of the over-thirty generation that places too much emphasis on the unusual appearance of the rock stars themselves, or their behavior.

All well and good if these are true, but are they? Are these assertions justified? Let us find out! We have already dealt with the Beatles and the advent of their amplified sound in Hamburg. Let us turn to the concept of multimedia experiences, and see how the supersalesmen of the record industry are willing to try to persuade us that combined rock, sex, and drug experiences are beneficial.

At the height of their success, major "rock ballrooms," like the Fillmore, attracted audiences by the thousands. Discotheques had walls covered with a variety of fast-changing psychedelic lights.

These forms of entertainment or amusement are inevitably heightened by indulgence in drugs. Alvin Toffler, in *Future Shock*, has described these experiences as products based on "simulated environments that offer the customer a taste of adventure, danger, sexual titillation or other pleasures without risk to his real life or reputation." Toffler goes on to describe projected creation of various experimental enclaves capable of re-creating, through technological imagination, any artificial environment ranging from the Roman splendor of ancient times to the social atmosphere of the royal courts of European or Oriental potentates. These "experiential environments" will offer an opportunity for the customer to enjoy artificial, simulated experiences by participating in a planned sequence of events designed by an alliance of museum experts and Madison Avenue publicists and intended to provide temporary transport to other times and places. Toffler goes on to describe an "electronic studio of participation" in Manhattan, where guests in semitransparent robes dance to rock music, and they are provided with stereophonic headsets, see-through masks, and an assortment of balloons, kaleidoscopes, tambourines, plastic pillows, mirrors, pieces of crystal, marshmallows, slides, and a slide projector. Obviously, getting one's "kicks" has become a highly sophisticated procedure.

Advocates of the counterculture make an enormous issue of

words like "honesty" and "relevance." White, middle-American suburbia is a symbol of cultural backwardness. Reality, we are told, is what counts! Rock festivals are identified as a return to nature, an escape from the plasticized existence of the typical American family. But the counterculture advocates cannot have it both ways. If they are opposed to escapism from truth, from reality, they are entitled to their view. But they ridicule the families that visit Disneyland, all the while lamenting the demise of their own medium of escape, the Fillmore. Having one's ideological cake and eating it too is thoroughly respectable in the counterculture.

Discussions of the groups and their leaders invariably turn to their communal life-style and the musician-listener rapport established through mutual participation in rock and drugs. What is this life-style?

One basic assumption, to which even critics of "rock" have subscribed, is that the "rock group" is by definition "anti-Establishment." This is a highly emotional term, implying that the protesting group or individual enjoys an "outsider" identity. Most contemporary pop musicians claim to ridicule the values of the vague power structure which is resented by all, defined as the Establishment. Initially, it is true that rock music found its aesthetic roots in teenage rebellion. But we must ask ourselves, against what were the teenagers rebelling? High school? Homework? Restrictions on dating? What are today's rock fans seeking? Although the groups of the late 1960's and early 1970's allegedly were protesting the Vietnam War, the actions of the army, against pollution, against their parents and society in general, and against those who do not agree with them, they have had no difficulty finding a forum.

Which establishment are these groups opposing? Are they opposed to Mike Curb, President of MGM Records? Are they opposed to his colleagues at the other record companies and motion picture studios, who welcome them with open arms? Are they opposed to the newspapers which give their concerts as much attention as recitals by Horowitz or Heifetz? Does the Establishment (i.e., the critics, the business executives, the academicians, the big corporations, etc.) really oppose their anti-Establishment posture? Hardly, because youth-oriented executives who favor a commercialized culture dominated by teenage taste have purged or fired those who disagree. It's all right, we must understand, to talk about revolution and burning down the Establishment, so long as the buildings burned belong to the Bank of America or the United States government, and not any major record companies. It's just dandy to write protest songs about private property, so long as the property to be confiscated doesn't happen to belong to any of the major record producers.

Steve Lawrence, one of the few commercially successful performers to criticize the executives in public has observed, "The network executives tell you the level of their audience is twelve to sixteen years of age. Record executives try to reach a market between nine and fourteen. They play down to people instead of playing up." He also points out that the executives regularly develop policies based on the assumption that, "If it's good, it won't sell."

In truth, the anti-Establishment label has become fashionable in a society that caters to the youth cult. The record industry regards the "destruction of the Establishment" as the latest trend, in the tradition of beach parties and blue suede shoes of yesteryear. It is ironic that while pseudo-intellectual supporters are praising the rock groups as anti-Establishment, they are enjoying the enthusiastic support of film and television executives, the recording industry executives, the academic fraternity, members of the intelligentsia who regard such support as fashionable, and even the veritable army of critics who turn out column after column explaining the identification of rock groups with the poor and disenfranchised of the world.

Consider the words of Ralph J. Gleason, former jazz critic, now self-proclaimed "rock freak," who observes solemnly: "Implicit in the very names of the business organizations that these youths form is an attack on the traditional, serious attitude toward money." After praising the imagery in choices of such names as the Jefferson Airplane and the Grateful Dead, Gleason goes on to explain, "Attacking the conventional attitude toward money is considered immoral in the society of our fathers, because money is sacred. The reality of what Bob Dylan says—'Money doesn't talk, it swears'—has yet to seep through."

A prime example of this disdain for money is a young man named James Brown. Brown, who is considered a representative of Black Pride, is a soul singer. He expresses the role of the black man in rock, but his works are intended to be understood by persons of all races, especially those who identify with poverty and humility.

James Brown, widely recognized as the most successful "soul" singer, is a case in point. Brown, a spokesman for the poor and disenfranchised, travels with a uniformed chauffeur. He has a three-car garage, a purple Cadillac limousine, a red Stingray with "Mr. Dynamite" painted on the side, and a white Cadillac. Brown has been known to use 1000 pairs of cufflinks a month, which he tosses to the audience during his performances. His wardrobe consists of 120 glistening shirts, slacks, capes, and eighty pairs of shoes and boots. He is surrounded by a managerial staff that attends to his needs. On tour, he is preceded by a team of interior decorators who redesign the hotel rooms he will occupy, especially to suit his taste. Once, James Brown was very poor. Now, however, he leads a life-style which Ralph Gleason believes is irreverent in regard to money. Protest is profitable in the 1970's.

It is easy enough to declare that the philosophies of the rock stars as expressed in their lyrics may differ with the attitudes exemplified by their life-styles. But if this is true, they are hypocrites and should be treated accordingly. Nik Cohn recalled a conversation with Bert Berns, an active pop songwriter. He asked Berns to explain what pop was about. Berns responded by turning around, and summoning a waiter to their table. Cohn commented, "Immediately, three waiters burst out of the wings at a canter and dashed to our table. Berns asked for a match and was faced by a sudden wall of flame, by three flickering hands. When the waiters left, Berns looked at me and wasn't even smug about it. 'Wouldn't you say?' he asked, 'That's what pop's about.' "

Mick Jagger, leader of the Rolling Stones, who has an irreverent perspective on the subject of financial profit, is known to maintain a dark blue Aston Martin, an eleven-bedroom house in Hampshire with butler's cottage and man-made lake, and a town house in

Chelsea. The former is evaluated at £25,000 and the latter at £45,000. Elvis Presley lives on an estate in Tennessee large enough to accommodate indoor roller skating. Sonny and Cher, the husband and wife team, recently purchased a palatial California estate from film star Tony Curtis. The list is endless. A record company called Coed Records went to Federal Court, proposing that payola should be a legalized business exemption on income tax. If the "myth" of "irreverence toward money" helps to build an anti-Establishment image, all to the good, so far as the rock-promoters are concerned. But the rock groups never forget that a major publication devoted to their efforts is appropriately named, *Cashbox*. This is really tracing rock to its roots.

We now turn to consideration of the life-style of these rock groups, a life-style with which young persons who have achieved Charles Reich's Consciousness III are expected to sympathize.

Reich suggests that "the use of drugs, especially because they are illegal, establishes a blood brotherhood before the musicians even begin to play." The same could be said for holding up a bank or committing other assorted crimes. Imagine the outrage heard from the public if a respected social critic were to suggest that a troupe of actors or dancers establish a blood brotherhood by burning all the existing copies of *The Greening of America*. While this might be considered a public service in some circles, it seems logical that thoughtful, sensible Americans would oppose such actions as illegal and immoral; it would seem that they would oppose a blood brotherhood based on violation of the drug laws for the same reason. Perhaps Charles Reich would agree, but he does not choose to tell us.

John Lennon, who modestly asserted that the Beatles were more popular than Jesus, has offered a description of the Beatles' life-style at the height of their success.

"The Beatles tours were like the Fellini film *Satirycon*," he declared, acknowledging free use of girls, marijuana, LSD, and heroin. "Wherever we went, there was always a whole scene going, we had four separate bedrooms." When pressed by a reporter as to how the group managed to keep its "clean image" during these tours, which he freely compared to Roman orgies, Lennon replied, "Everybody wants to keep on the bandwagon of

free women, liquor and fun." Is this the idealistic life-style based
on a new sense of values publicized by the apologists for rock
groups? In truth, these values are no different from the values
which dominate any corrupt society. Are the morals of John
Lennon different from those of Willie Stark, the ambitious political
boss of *All the King's Men*? Are they more sensitive or idealistic
than the values which dominated the lives of the entourage which
surrounded Al Capone? Are they less hedonistic than the whimsical pursuits of pleasure and instant gratifications that existed at the
courts of Imperial Rome? Are they more honest than those of
fawning Uriah Heep, plotting and scheming, while protesting to
the public that he is a clerk known to all as 'umble Uriah?

John Lennon is not unique among the Beatles in this respect,
just as the Beatles are not unique among rock groups. These young
men and women, projected into positions of importance and
wealth far beyond their achievements, receive the adoration of the
masses. Like wolves in sheep's clothing, they enjoy the advantages
and pleasures of an amoral existence while chastising conservative
society as a social conscience. Their promiscuous, irresponsible
life-style is based on instant gratification; they cannot fail to serve
their whims, because the usual values which affect the lives of
stronger men are irrelevant to their material existences. Like
spoiled children, they indulge themselves, while their middle-aged
press agents (and academic apologists) applaud their discovery of a
life-style that is as old as corruption itself, and as morally jaded.

Some also suggest the rock group as the ideal example of
cooperative brotherhood. This, of course, is utter nonsense, as
anyone vaguely familiar with the legal relationships between
group members will affirm. Paul McCartney went to court to have
the Beatles legally dissolved; McCartney also asked the courts to
appoint financial managers to take control of the money earned by
the Beatles during the years they were enjoying their spirit of
brotherhood for fun and profit. Lennon, not to be outdone, insisted
that he, not McCartney, had been the first to abandon the group.

Most of the Beatles' legal problems are not unique, however.
Many of the rock groups engage in various kinds of legal intrigues.
Often it is because one member of the group, like the Supremes'
Diana Ross, is ambitious enough to try to become a superstar on

her own. The rock groups sue their managers; they often sue each other. Recently, a prominent Hollywood manager, preferring to remain anonymous, recalled a friend of his, a San Francisco promoter, who experienced some of the brotherhood of the rock groups. He found a group of nomadic youngsters in the Haight-Ashbury section of San Francisco. The manager bought them a group of musical instruments, taught them elementary guitar chords, because they were musically illiterate, purchased costumes, paid their rent, and went to work promoting a public image. The group, exemplifying the spirit of brotherhood described by rock-music critics, promptly took their manager to court. They sued and won.

In the 1960's, the nature of pop-music lyrics changed radically. The early rock lyrics had been derivative of country-and-western subjects (i.e., Presley's "Hound Dog") and scaled the heights of teenage inanity with the Beatles' "I Want to Hold Your Hand." Gradually, however, pop music began to absorb those influences of the high-school and college cultures which were growing like giant weeds. A high-school coed would hardly worry about being sweet sixteen if she were primarily concerned about her alleged right to get an abortion. Crew-cuts and football had been replaced by the "right" to take LSD. The youth cult, with its emphasis on free love (or more appropriately, free sex), drugs, and revolution, was making itself heard. Bob Dylan became a well-known figure in pop music, and the Beatles started turning to social and political subjects. For the first time, rock music and lyrics were acquiring artistic pretensions. Previously, the total lack of quality, the obvious bad music and bad lyrics, had been a selling point to teenage audiences. A curious interaction between pop musicians and journalists came into play. The journalists were eager to advance their own theories about Vietnam, abortion, drugs, long hair, and a variety of social issues. The presence of influential and very rich songwriters who trumpeted their own views was convenient. Advocates of the counterculture could point to the success of "rock music" with its protest lyrics as a justification for their own political programs, candidates, and ambitions. The rock groups (and their promoters) could draw upon critical acclaim as a publicity device.

Eager to find the "poignant, eloquent voices of youthful protest" which the journalists and pseudo-intellectuals decided had to be found somewhere in the younger generation, they turned to the rock groups. If the music was unmusical, if the lyrics were crude, no matter—not so long as the social and political views matched their own interpretation of the political events at hand. The result was an almost comical situation; the rock composers and lyricists were credited with the most unbelievable political and social profundity. The "intellectuals" echoed the views of the rock groups who echoed the views of the intellectuals.

The journalists and professors, eager to reinforce their own preconceived notions about the younger generation, conveniently neglected those young men and women who did not subscribe to the social or political views espoused by the rock groups. Instead, they waited eagerly for the rock composers and lyricists, now armed with their new-found academic respectability, to sit down in their elegant mansions, set aside their furs, jewels, and Rolls-Royces, and write the weekly protest.

But rock music and lyrics had never before been accepted as anything but teenage music. Now the counterculture was offering its self-styled "philosophy" as the viewpoint of the younger generation. Even high-school newspapers had become involved in controversies over the alleged "right" to take drugs or to print obscenities in school publications. Gradually, publishers and record companies became more and more permissive, welcoming each new four-letter word or suggestive reference to drugs or sex in the lyrics as a crusade. Suddenly the record industry, like an intoxicated octopus, began the inevitable search to find something more shocking or controversial than ever before. It didn't have to look very far.

Rock music had always attracted the strange and bizarre; it was one of the few fields of endeavor in which one could become a superstar, with all the trappings of fame and wealth, without any special talents or skills, save the ability to choose the right manager. A careful study of the lyrics of hit songs reveals no special insights; rather, we find lyrics which happened to be on the right (or should we say *left*) side of the political fence.

The ultimate philosophical statement of the counterculture was supposed to be the American tribal love-rock musical, *Hair.* Written by Gerome Ragni and James Rado, and produced under the auspices of Joseph Papp, *Hair* had something for everyone. By wrapping itself in the mantle of youth, *Hair* could glory in its amateurism and eschew any claims of professionalism. *Hair* was promoted as a celebration, a show full of love, the best that the young people of this country had to offer. The lyrics, admittedly, were primitive, but the critics wanted to be understanding. The kids, we were told, meant well, as they sang, "Let it fly in the breeze and get caught in the trees, give a home to the fleas in my hair."

Hair had no plot, in the sense of a formal book-musical. Instead, it consisted of a deafening, amplified revue of rock songs, a cast kept constantly in motion, writhing and twisting to the music. A loosely constructed story-line about a young man named "Claude" tied the songs together. Claude, it seems, had been drafted, and the prospect of giving up all he held dearly, most especially his flea-infested hair, a ready supply of marijuana, the right to swear in mixed company, and a girl friend who believed in free and easy sex, was too much to bear. *Hair* gloried in its primitive crudity, virtually daring the critics to dislike it. Realistically, it should have been received as a poorly conceived musical, with no book, ineffectively crude lyrics, and non-music. Instead, the critics purred. Clive Barnes, writing in the *New York Times,* called the show, "Sweet, subtle, and sheer fun." Much of the attention focused on a scene in which members of the cast, wearing absolutely nothing at all, faced the audience on a dimly lighted stage. Critical reaction varied. One observer said that when nudity came to Broadway, "All those Scarsdale ladies got to look at a strange man's bottom."

Hair offered the youth cult and portrayed it exactly as it really is: dirty, crude, vulgar, and concerned primarily with sex, drugs, indulgence, and self-gratification. If *Hair* had been on the other side of the political fence, it is doubtful that the critics would have been so solicitous. If *Hair* had been a Cohan-style review which waved the flag and presented a parade of soldiers marching across the stage, the critics would have screamed. They would have turned their venom upon a lyricist who dared to write using such a primitive rhyme as "Timothy Leary, dearie." But the critical reception for *Hair* was, in microcosm, the reaction to the whole rock-music phenomenon. The critics will not howl in dismay if the subject in question is wrapped in the mantle of protest, because this reinforces the critics' own notion of the younger generation.

As time has gone on, the political and social perspective of rock music has moved farther and farther to the left. There is nothing to be gained by listing the assorted obscenities and four-letter words which have been used in pop lyrics. There are no taboos. Rock lyrics glorified the drug culture until public protest forced minimal curtailment. The new underground groups were pictured as so "new" and "exciting" and "electrifying" as to make yesterday's groups seem tame. From one social and political tangent to another, the trends have played ideological hopscotch, finally turning toward the violent, obscene, and emotionally ill. If Elvis Presley suggested the idea of sex, the new groups or the leaders wouldn't bother with simple suggestions. If the Beatles' long hair seemed effeminate to the men who wore crew-cuts in the 1950's, the new groups would go one step farther.

The result has not been a coherent political or social philosophy, or even a set of skillfully written lyrics or musically inspired tunes. Instead, society has been offered a freak show. Michel Polnareff, a French pop-singer, appears in a woman's hat, frilly blouse, with his own backside bare. An advertisement for the Edgar Winter Group pictured a person with alabaster skin, white hair, dark lipstick, bare shoulders, and a silver necklace. Nationally syndicated columnist, Art Seidenbaum, remarked, "Only the prominent Adam's apple suggested that this mysterious creature is a man." Seidenbaum also refers to rock-star, David Bowie, as, "an artist of imprecise sex who deliberately blurs the fine line between that which is male and that which is female."

In recent months, rock audiences have become so accustomed to the sick, the bizarre, the violent, and the obscene, that promoters are forced to seek new depths of depravity in order to hit the Top Forty. By catering to the most abnormal elements of a society, businessmen can always find some new curiosity to be advertised as a thrill. But they offer us a sick, violent, obscene exhibition, not the idyllic wholesome, expression of "America's young people," that slick salesmen would have us believe.

In today's culture, rock is taken seriously. It is reviewed in magazines that are considered "intellectual fare." Universities offer courses in rock music. Wiley Housewright, former President of the Music Educators National Conference, has urged that rock be introduced in the public schools as a means of "communicating" with students of elementary school age.

What are the aesthetics of rock? For an answer, it is best to turn to primary sources, the young men and women who create rock themselves. Frank Zappa is the leader of a musical aggregation known as the Mothers of Invention. Because he has attended college, he is generally accepted as one of the aesthetic spokesmen of the rock movement; in any event, he is advertised as such. Zappa likes to suggest that he is a satirist. He is ridiculing society, and trying to take an ironic view of life in general, including the youth culture. But Zappa went so far as to produce an album entitled "We're Only in it for the Money." Perhaps the academic apologists deserve Zappa, but unfortunately, the rest of society must tolerate his creative efforts as well. Zappa demonstrated his capacity to be the spokesman for the aesthetics of rock when he had himself photographed sitting on the toilet.

Zappa explained to Sally Kempton the aesthetic background of the group: "We were playing at local beer joints for like six dollars a night. I finally decided this would not do, so I began calling up all the clubs in the area. This was in 1965, and to get work you had to sound like the Beatles or the Rolling Stones." (Observe the anti-Establishment Beatles and Stones who had everyone against them!) Zappa goes on. "You also had to have long hair and due to an unfortunate circumstance all my hair had been cut off. I used to tell club managers that we sounded exactly like the Rolling Stones. Anyway we finally got a booking in a club in Pomona, and were something of a hit. It was more because of our act than because of our music. People used to go away and tell their friends that here was this group that insulted the audience." (It is easy to see why Frank Zappa grew long hair; he obviously wanted to be a "non-conformist.")

Zappa's efforts prevailed. "Then MGM sent someone around to sign us to a contract. Their guy came into the club during a set of 'Brain Police' and he said, 'Aha, a protest rhythm and blues group,' so they paid us accordingly. The fee we got for signing was incredibly small, particularly considering the number of guys in the group."

We see no sense of bitter social protest, no sense of ideological outrage, no sense of passionate desires to break with the established goals of society. What we see, as expressed in the words of a leading member of the musical movement described by many as our new cultural, social conscience is that Frank Zappa wanted to make money, to be successful (in the conventional, materialistic sense). Social protest was considered to be commercially viable by the commercial promoters, and Frank Zappa was happy to oblige.

Zappa's career rose steadily; he now runs his own advertising agency, which presumably helped to publicize a concert which featured the Mothers of Invention and the Los Angeles Philharmonic in a work especially written by Zappa, to be conducted by the regular symphony musical director, Zubin Mehta. The site of this concert was Pauley Pavilion, home of the UCLA basketball dynasty. To make the concert respectable, the Philharmonic also added a new electronic composition written for orchestra and tape recorder by Mel Powell, of Yale, the 1940's dance bands, and now Dean of the School of Music at California Institute of the Arts. Powell, after a technical breakdown resulting from a faulty cable prevented completion of the performance of his piece, decided that his work could not receive serious attention. He tried to leave the auditorium, declining another attempt at performance because Zappa's group had taken over the stage. His exit was blocked by the mercurial Ernest Fleischmann, manager and executive director of the Philharmonic. When he saw that Powell was determined to leave the auditorium, Fleischmann responded by promising that Powell would never again receive a performance of his work by the Philharmonic. Powell, justifiably furious, struck home in his denunciation of the pseudo-intellectual rationale employed by apologists for much of today's current pop music. He also explained the rapport, the feeling of kindred spirit that exists between rock groups and their audiences.

Powell declares: "Minimal musical awareness informs us that there isn't an instrumental, vocal, or compositional entity presented nowadays by the majority of rock groups to their millions of devotees that is so much as an inch beyond the reach of an utterly unaccomplished amateur. Except for the handful of genuinely gifted in this field, its profession becomes a form of participatory democracy in which the talentless kid in his living room plunking away on his guitar idolizes the equally talentless kid on the tube or recording, plunking away on his guitar. If the medium is the message, the message here is that the medium is an ego trip mirror; it scarcely matters who is transmitting, who is receiving." Powell has correctly identified the dangers of applying egalitarian attitudes to evaluation of the arts.

"Doing one's own thing" has become a convenient excuse for a lack of creative talent or imagination. Because pop music is offered as "people's music," we seem almost eager to excuse the fact that the performers have little to offer. It may be very well for a performer to simply "do his own thing" but if he's doing it on national television or in Carnegie Hall, one hopes he is capable of carrying a tune or playing more than five chords on his guitar.

The result is the usual obliteration of values and debunking of excellence which has become the curse of the glorified youth culture. Powell observes, "The rule then becomes either Beethoven was black or he wasn't beautiful. Mozart does his thing, and so does Ringo. Man it's the same, don't you dig? Bach and those cats got their own scene just like Snooty Sam and the Father-Grabbing Anti-Oinkers got their own scene." Powell concludes with the comment, "An immediate consequence of this conceptual garbage is the commercial exploitation of genuinely well-intentioned young innocents whose deep devotion to social justice somehow renders them so vulnerable to music-hustling demagogues." What Powell has realized, and what others do not, is that intelligent, well-meaning people, in their desire to bend over backward to be receptive to creative work which is advertised as youth-oriented, may check their common sense (and their taste, if they have any) at the door when they try to evaluate rock concerts. Zappa, explaining some of his aesthetic ideas, recalls, "It was very tough getting the group together in the beginning. A lot of guys didn't want to submit to our packaging. They didn't like making themselves ugly, but they especially didn't like playing ugly." Zappa's techniques of orchestration are unusual to say the least. "I found some violins in a closet and I gave them to three of the guys. None of them had ever played a violin before. They were making all these weird sounds on them."

It is common knowledge in the music industry that a guitar, knowledge of a few chords, and a gullible, willing public, are enough to create rock stars if the manager or promoter does his job. Of course, it is always advisable to prepackage such performing artists, employing a publicity campaign. Ideally, they should claim to express profound aesthetic meanings in their work, fashionably related to the popular political trends of the day. Critics, academics, and some of the public like to think that rock is treated as a serious art form. Pontification and pretentiousness are customarily greeted with glee.

Frank Zappa, advertising executive in behalf of his own work, expressed amusement that MGM Records objected to certain lyrics of his which the company felt could be interpreted as obscene. Zappa's response was to indicate that war and other public ills were his idea of bad taste.

This is a classic case of *non sequitur*. Why does the existence of social ills justify bad taste or obscenity, on the part of Zappa or anyone else? Zappa, of course, can defend himself by saying that standards of taste and obscenity are relative. The concept of shifting, relative standards is fashionable today, because cultural anarchy thrives on the notion that there are no fixed standards of taste or beauty. Although individual styles have varied for years among composers, writers, and artists, great masterworks of art have exhibited certain common traits that overlap the beginnings and endings of eras. (In music, the capacity to write beautiful melody is a case in point.)

One standard objection to criticism of rock groups is the assertion that closed minds (or ears) may overlook the work of a neglected genius. Critics inevitably remind us of Eduard Hanslick, the musical reviewer who ridiculed the innovations of Wagner in the late nineteenth century. Like all reasonable principles, open-mindedness can be carried too far. At one time, courts handed down harsh sentences; today, many Americans believe that the courts are permissive and inclined to favor the criminal. A similar situation exists in music. Certain critics are so afraid of failing to recognize another Wagner that they may accept a performer who bangs two tin cans together as a virtuoso. The poet who mumbles incoherently or shouts obscenities at an audience is accepted because the critics are afraid of becoming known as the men who failed to identify another Keats.

Another familiar argument raised suggests that a performance by a contemporary musician or singer must be judged within its own context. But this too can lead us astray; if the large majority of such performers cannot sing or play well, the untalented mediocrity is elevated to star status because he is compared with his even less talented rivals.

The concept of uniform standards does not propose our evaluation of contemporary art by antiquated standards. But we can be careful enough not to create an elite class of artists whose work cannot be criticized, under the sanctuary of a modern label. Bad musicianship and incoherence cannot be overlooked in the works of self-styled modernists, especially when these standards are applied to everyone else.

Critics try to analyze and explain the lyrics of rock groups as "poetry." Unfortunately, middle-aged apologists for the rock culture blithely assume that rock lyrics are profound. Yet the widely criticized "Sergeant Pepper," analyzed by all the major critics and commentators, is a prime example of what is wrong with intellectual rock criticism. Paul McCartney describes the choice of title in these words: "I was just thinking of nice words like 'Sergeant Pepper and Lonely Hearts Club,' and they came together for no reason." The poetry which critics praise espouses the political and social attitudes of the self-styled cultural revolution. We shall shortly examine some of these attitudes to determine whether or not they are really profound. Perhaps a prime example of this philosophy is the lyric by the Jefferson Airplane, that declares, "We are obscene, lawless, hideous, dangerous, dirty, violent, and young." These revolutionary lyrics also inform us, "We are all outlaws in the eyes of Amerika. In order to survive, we steal, cheat, lie, forge, ⎯⎯⎯⎯⎯, hide and deal." (Obscenity not printed.)

The Rolling Stones sing, "The time is ripe for violent revolution." John Coyne suggests, "Visit Berkeley and look at the kids, the young ones. Junior-high-school girls with eyes as knowing and dead as any prostitute's. They've had it all, they know things at thirteen that we didn't learn until our twenties. They've experienced it all, years before they were mentally ready, and by the late teens they're jaded. They never will get any satisfaction, for they've experienced it before they should, and then they reach the age at which they're mentally ready, it's behind them."

When these "poets" are not praising revolution, they are praising involvement with drugs, another subject to be dealt with shortly. Charles Manson, convicted mass-murderer, has recorded a rock album in prison. The major rock groups do not deny that their records are enveloped in subtle analogies and double meanings, all propagandizing for the drug culture.

Surprisingly enough, the most curious reaction to the efforts of these groups has come from middle-class and affluent Americans. Rock is socially "in." We can hear it at the best parties. Some of our most famous musical figures have endorsed it as a serious art form.

To understand this, we must remember that the culture revolution which has occurred at a lightning-fast pace has affected adults as well as children. When we speak of rock as the music of the "young," we must remember that many of these "youngsters" are over thirty. Society is fashionable for the young. Like Br'er Rabbit's briar patch, the old is unthinkable. People cannot stand aging in a society which increasingly reduces the minimal age of acceptance in a social definition of youth. Alvin Toffler, in *Future Shock*, speaks of a frustrated nine-year-old who had never been to Europe. Her life seemed meaningless because she felt she had nothing left to experience in the world but a trip to Europe. If a nine-year-old can react this way, should it surprise us that many fathers and mothers regard their children as *youth symbols to be followed and imitated* rather than the other way around? When a man reaches forty, he is at the dangerous age. He may have teenage children; he desires their approval, their affection, most of all, he desires a reaffirmation of his own youth, which is contradictory to the reality of his children.

Many of these men, some of them very distinguished, are faced with long-haired, unwashed, teenage children, trying to organize rock groups, to participate in the new youth culture. Can a man publicly express his feelings about the "new sound" when his children are part of the teenage population creating that sound? Some men can; but some cannot, and these men do society a disservice because they lend a prestige and a respectability to ideas and persons who would never be taken seriously otherwise.

Leonard Bernstein, recognized by everyone as a brilliant, creative man, with an aura of glamor that lends special credence to his opinions in the eyes of some, has endorsed rock. He says it is irresistible. He has written a mass which employs rock idioms. John Green, noted composer-conductor in the film industry, says he does not sympathize with persons who "won't even listen" to the Rolling Stones. John Lindsay, the charismatic idol of youth-oriented politics, leaps upon the stage to applaud the premiere of *Jesus Christ, Superstar.* This is a rock opera intending to portray the life of Christ in new, "mod," "youthful," "rock" terms. All of these men lend their respectability to "rock." There are hundreds of others. They find nothing incongruous in the suggestion that the life of Christ may be portrayed in an idiom which is amoral, and enveloped in a Dionysian sub-culture of psychedelic hallucinations and psychological rationalization. They find nothing objectionable in the assertion that the soul of American political expression is best exemplified by the public exhibitionism of the late Jim Morrison, who, in the words of writer Joan Didion, "wore black vinyl pants and no underwear and tended to suggest some range of the possible just beyond a suicide pact." They are not frightened or dismayed because Morrison, arrested for indecent exposure, defined the group's interests as "anything about revolt, disorder, chaos about activity that appears to have no meaning."

They are not worried about the prospect that a generation of children, spoon-fed on comic-book culture and spoiled beyond our wildest imaginations, will soon be able to spend part of their daily school hour becoming indoctrinated in the myth that prepackaged "rock" is culture. If these men are concerned, or outraged, or disturbed, they are keeping it to themselves. A distinguished European film composer was summarily dismissed from his Hollywood contract because he was not considered "a viable commercially exploitable writer" despite his shelf of Academy Awards and wide critical acclaim.

Perhaps the most bizarre aspect of all in the rock revolution is the establishment of the vocal and physical freaks as the darlings of the jet set. (Social observers have shifted in their descriptive terms from jet set to Beautiful People to the current "Cat Pack.") Artistic patronage has always been fashionable for the wealthy; Haydn had Prince Metternich, Tschaikowsky had Mme. Meck, and it should not surprise us that patrons of all ages, shapes, and sizes have appeared to exert influence in contemporary music as well. But a hallmark of such activities was always the artistic skill and sophistication of the persons being assisted. The sight of New York's social and literary circles engaged in an almost masochistic pursuit of the non-musicians and non-poets of the counterculture is peculiar. Nik Cohn has commented, "Why pop? Because the yen was all for youth and beauty, and if nothing else, pop was always young, always beautiful. Because pop made its money for itself. Because it spoke so coarse ('Common as dirt, darlings, isn't he divine?'). Because it was what's happening, baby doll. What more reason does anyone need?"

Thus, in what may be the oddest twist of all, the rich, famous, and socially prominent turn for a status symbol to lower classes, to the coarseness and vulgarity of a teenage culture gone wrong. The ultimate status symbol, we are told, was to be snubbed by the Beatles or a pouting Mick Jagger, all during the 1960's. In the 1970's, there are new stars ready to accept the plaudits of a worshipful social élite. Occasionally, however, victims of the rock revolution express themselves in private.

A studio music executive, middle-aged and nervously expecting a purge from his twenty- to thirty-year-old superiors, praised the "new sound in his office." Then, speaking to the author in private, he confided, "They've created a monster, and it's going to destroy us." The word has been handed down. The "do your own thing" rock groups have taken over. They express their brotherhood, their love of humanity, and their self-respect by behaving in the most degrading ways capable of emanating from human imagination. Non-rock musicians need not apply.

Amid this commercial society, which behaves with the spirit of brotherly love found at any medieval court, we hear the critics and academics, afraid of being left behind. Charles Reich, a forty-two-year-old Yale Professor of Law with long sideburns declares, deferentially, "It is no criticism of the eighteenth- or nineteenth-century geniuses to say that today's music has found a world they never knew." He goes on to describe the over-amplified, ear-deafening montage of writhing, screaming, agonizing rock groups and their mass-mob psychologically captive audience as providing "greater energy than Beethoven's Ninth."

Critics of these middle-aged men, longing for the nostalgia of a young image in the mirror, are dismissed as old fogies. Spiro Agnew denounces the relationship between rock and drugs. William F. Buckley, Jr. observes that the Beatles commit "non-music." Calvin Jackson proposes that "a Beatle is something you step on—quick." The youth cult, with its conformist dress and conformist, blind adherence to the dictates of *Billboard* and *Cashbox*, insisting that it dislikes labels, dismisses these criticisms. Charles G. Rousculp, a high-school teacher and writer, who was Ohio's teacher of the year, counsels, "Adults help the teen businesses along by assuring a constant turnover in teen styles. The cry today is, 'I'd rather be young than be President.' As soon as adults have 'moved in' in their pathetic desire to be teenagers, too, the teenage industries discard the Twist, the Total Look, the 'Yeah–Yeah–Yeah,' or whatever it is, and produce a new teenage something or other. And so the cycle proceeds."

And as the cycle proceeds, the academics and propagandists prepare to draw upon their credentials and their jargon to create a social and ethical basis for the greatest commercial fraud of the twentieth century, possibly in the history of Western civilization.

Rock advocates see the social, cultural, artistic work of the rock groups, and praise their sensitivity, their false morality, their hypocritical life-style, and their imaginary technical competency. There are hundreds ready to follow the false gods of the rock world. Lest we forget, remember the words of Fabulous Fabian, teenage idol of yesteryear, now mature ex-star trying to find a place for himself in a world he is trying to understand: "I was created."

And then recall another Colonel Parker, of another time and place, who said, "A sucker was born every minute, and two to fleece him." Finally, think of Abraham Lincoln, who suggested, "You can fool some of the people all of the time, and all of the people some of the time, but you can't fool all of the people all of the time." Then turn on the radio, the television, the record player, or try "communicating" with your local neighborhood teenager. The youth cult, and its high priests, the rock groups, like the men who designed the Emperor's New Clothes, are ready for you!

IV.
The Drug Mystique:
Invitation to Suicide

If the apologists for the youth culture may be forgiven their ignorance of the fact that rock music is as commercial a commodity as automobiles or toothpaste, they cannot escape so easily when they turn to the drug mystique, a collection of attitudes and ideas that have already been discussed at length in the newspapers and on radio and television. It is embarrassing to argue against the drug mystique; it is equivalent to being asked to explain why earthquakes are unpleasant or why murder should be illegal. But in a day and age when even the obvious may be challenged, it is necessary to do exactly that. The academics and political figures who chastise their contemporaries for not "really listening" to the unwashed creations of *Cashbox* and *Billboard*, are entitled to their taste. If they believe that the soul of American conscience is best expressed by a quartet of feeble-looking males wearing shoulder-length hair, with robust voices worthy of anemic victims of consumption, it is their privilege.

But when they turn to the subject of drugs, they are dealing with a subject which can be analyzed in terms of hard facts and scientific evidence—evidence which condemns them overwhelmingly as men whose desire for the approval of irresponsible youth obliterates what remaining common sense they have.

Within the last several years, a curious aggregation of high-school and college students, professors, politicians, dropouts and militants, have combined forces in an incredible campaign to proselytize and advertise the drug culture. Drugs have been portrayed as a medium capable of solving all society's problems at once, in terms worthy of a 1910 melodrama. Predictably, the villains of the piece are those scientists or social leaders who regard the use of drugs not as a way to find God or a journey beyond the rainbow, but as a Pandora's box. When thrown open, the box offers a variety of evils capable of dealing death to those foolish enough to believe the propaganda. Pseudo-mature academics and "intellectuals" have been willing to lend the prestige of their social and scholarly positions to a drug culture that can only be deemed suicidal by sane men in search of the truth. Let us examine some facts.

Much of the public's attention has focused upon disagreements over the legalization or decriminalization of marijuana. No longer an isolated problem affecting a single group or age bracket in society, marijuana, or "pot," to use the vernacular, is all over the newspapers. News media have reported instances of students of elementary and junior-high-school age turning to marijuana.

Advocates of pot portray its use as a harmless, spiritual experience with few ill effects. Some persons insist that there is no relationship between marijuana and the use of hard drugs. Others have attempted to persuade us that even such drugs as LSD are a means of pursuing enlightened truth. A large contingent of the academic community is all too eager to sneer and laugh nervously at the insensitive Establishment which conspires to deny progressive adults and their children their truth serum. We may consider the questions of marijuana and other drugs separately, although they are related in many ways. Conclusions should always be based on hard, cold, dispassionate scientific evidence. We turn to the medical and scientific experts for the true facts.

Dr. Edward R. Pinckney, former editor of the *AMA Journal*, told writer Jess Stearn, "It is almost criminal for those so far from the field of medicine or pharmacology to be so dogmatic about something they know nothing about." Stearn has recounted the details of his lengthy investigations into the uses of marijuana and LSD in his book, *The Seekers*. Pinckney referred to a recent medical panel which described marijuana's effects: "postural hypotension (disturbance of normal blood pressure reflexes), mydriasis (excessive dilating of pupils), conjunctival congestion (bloodshot eyes) and frequent photophilia (affinity for light). Muscular incoordination, spasms, urinary frequency, dryness of mouth, nausea, vomiting, and diarrhea sometimes occur. Increase in appetite is common, and has been attributed to hypoglycemia (decrease of blood sugar). Hypothermia (lowered temperatures) has been observed, and some workers have noted a Raynaud-like syndrome (cold extremities and white fingertips). Large amounts of marijuana depress respiration, which is the first sign of impending death in animals given lethal doses." The panel also noted many alarming psychological and social changes. References may be found to panic, gross confusion, impulsive and aggressive behavior, depersonalization, depression, and paranoid behavior.

Dr. Luis Souza has presented a report to the Bergen County (N.J.) Narcotic Addiction and Drug Abuse Council suggesting chromosomal damage directly related to the use of marijuana. The American Medical Association has released a report linking marijuana to a psychological dependence capable of producing both emotional and physical ills; included in the physiological dangers were chronic bronchitis, asthma, low blood sugar, sleep disturbance, and impaired coordination.

Dr. Constandinos J. Miras of the University of Athens, and a Visiting Professor at UCLA, after twenty years of research, has concluded that significant use of marijuana may produce a psychologically lethargic state as a result of organic brain changes. His tests included evaluation of both humans and animals who had been exposed to large doses of marijuana. Dr. Harris Isbell of the University of Kentucky tested forty humans who used the drug and reported a variety of hallucinatory experiences. Admittedly, scientists have not completed their investigations into additional physiological dangers and psychological problems that may result from the use of this drug, but the list of difficulties which have already been directly related to marijuana is impressive.

Foremost among the difficulties encountered by the user of marijuana is psychological addiction. When the subject of drug addiction is raised, pro-drug spokesmen are quick to assure us that marijuana is non-addictive. Unfortunately, they do not bother to contend with the psychological effects of dependence upon marijuana.

Dr. Arthur H. Cain, psychologist and counselor, has outlined some of the aspects of psychological dependence upon marijuana in his highly informative book, *Young People and Drugs*. He observes that individuals who use pot regularly are less inclined to work or to learn. He goes on to comment, "This kind of learning simply cannot take place at age thirty;. it must occur during the teens or early twenties. If marijuana or any drug—inhibitors as they are of curiosity and learning, of intellectual, emotional, social, and spiritual growth—becomes even a part-time habit, the individual is going to reach the age when he should be assuming personal and social responsibilities in a condition wherein he is quite incapable of doing so because of his lack of growth in these essential areas."

Dr. Cain also declares, "I have never known a single teenager whom I could conscientiously declare sufficiently responsible for his own behavior, including behavior which might inflict personal damage, to entrust with even so mild a drug as marijuana."

In addition to physiological effects, the user of marijuana may become hilarious or careless; his judgment and memory may be affected. If his mood is inclined toward depression, he may become irritable or confused. Dr. Cain suggests that the mild euphoria of marijuana often serves to ease the guilt that may result from dropping out of society. In any event, dirt or filth are less unpleasant when the person surrounded by squalor is influenced by a drug. Psychologists consider the emotional defense of such drugs by their users to be a sign of addiction.

The report of the President's Commission on Marijuana has confused the issue further. Now, armed with the apparent sanction of a Presidential Commission, apologists for the youth cult are ready to declare pot as wholesome as apple pie. Before they do, they should prepare to deal with the hard questions, the unpleasant realities. These apologists do not choose to acknowledge the fact something is very wrong in a society (or youth sub-culture) which requires regular dependence upon drugs of any kind in order to remain happy or content. The Commission suggested relaxing penalties for private use of marijuana, while continuing to prosecute those who sell pot. Clearly, this is inconsistent. If it is wrong to sell something, it is also wrong to use that product.

Opponents of marijuana's legalization saw the Commission's work as an effort to appease advocates of the youth cult, to prove that the Commission was "progressive" and "reasonable." Advocates of drug use sneered at the Commission for "selling out" to the Establishment by acknowledging, in effect, that the Commission did not really object to private use of marijuana while objecting to public use or sale, at the same time. The President's Commission tried to please everyone, but pleased no one. Some traditionally conservative opponents of drugs have suggested that more time should be spent opposing the dangerous drugs, LSD and various narcotics and stimulants (i.e., amphetamines). But some critics of the Commission have denounced it as producing an unscientific document. Dr. Hardin B. Jones, Professor of Physiology at the University of California at Berkeley, who teaches classes in drug abuse, said that information used by the Commission was worded as if it had been written by potheads. The scientist declared, with reference to his studies of marijuana, that heroin users began their addiction with use of marijuana. He said that servicemen, whose psychological and behavioral patterns changed drastically as a result of heroin addiction, turned to the drug after initial experiences with marijuana. Law-enforcement officers were quick to recognize the legal and moral ambiguities in the commission report. Conservative spokesman, William F. Buckley, Jr., urged that marijuana laws be eased, referring to the research of Professor John Kaplan of Stanford and Professor Lester Grinspoon of Harvard. Kaplan opposed criminalization and Grinspoon suggested that marijuana does not harm the individual biologically or psychologically. Los Angeles District Attorney, Joseph P. Busch, declared, "Medical research into the habitual use of marijuana is highly inconclusive. Indications of liver damage, vascular brain damage, and ill effects on the immunity system and healing process—resulting from long-term use—have not been fully explored." The District Attorney went on to declare, "Yet [decriminalization] does not take into account the impact of stronger strains of marijuana, as have been observed in Vietnam, the powerful extracts of marijuana, and marijuana which is laced with powerful synthetic drugs such as DMT and TCP."

One is tempted to ask, "Which scientists should we believe?

Hardin Jones, Professor of Physiology and Anatomy at the University of California, Berkeley, suggests that marijuana causes brain damage and that "persons who use marijuana seem to have more deformed babies." Yet we are assured by a Presidential Commission that these assertions are less than valid. Perhaps in our efforts to understand political and social viewpoints from various "experts," we should keep in mind the observations of former drug addicts, young men and women who have escaped their former lives. Gail Bingham, who spent twelve of her twenty-five years as a drug addict, declared that conservative Republicans "won't be pushed into legalizing marijuana. They'll stand fast with the American way, with keeping the laws and not seeing them ripped out of the books." A twenty-one-year-old former heroin addict, Ed Mick, said, "We see different politicians trying to legalize marijuana for a few lousy votes. I don't care what they say about marijuana. It is harmful." The *Los Angeles Times* reported the establishment of a foundation for former drug addicts, ninety-five percent of whom favored doubling instead of lessening the penalties for using "pot." All of these former addicts began their drug experiences using marijuana.

Dr. Arthur H. Cain, noted author of books on the drug crisis, counseled young people to think of the future. He said, "Man and woman. These are two things you're never going to be if you remain on pot forever. All you'll ever be is a thirty-year-old baby hippie or a forty-year-old baby hippie, and I doubt very much that you'll live to be much older than that. You're stacking too many cards against a longer life every day you fool around with such chemicals and every moment that you continue to delude yourself that what you're doing is important."

The news media have generally emphasized those aspects of scientific discovery which may be favorable to marijuana. Certainly in recent months, many conservatives have chosen to rethink their own position with regard to pot. Richard C. Cowan, a member of the Young Americans for Freedom, writing in *National Review*, a leading journal of conservative opinion, went so far as to suggest that relaxing of the marijuana laws was an issue that should appeal to conservatives. He insisted that even those of us who take a dim view of the counterculture should revise our stands on marijuana. Cowan's arguments were essentially these: marijuana is non-addictive; it does not lead to the use of heroin; it does not induce criminal behavior, and in moderate effect, does not affect the driving or behavioral habits of persons who have no physical or mental-health problems.

These arguments have become fairly standard, even for those who otherwise oppose the cultural aberrations of the youth cult. But on this particular subject, these usually responsible conservatives seem eager to leap before they look. Dr. Harold Kolansky and Dr. William T. Moore, writing in the *AMA Journal*, reported that all thirty-eight patients who participated in their study of regular pot smoking were adversely affected. Eight became psychotic, four attempted suicide, thirteen unmarried girls became promiscuous, some with other girls and some with both sexes; of the latter, seven became pregnant. The two psychiatrists also reported that eighteen developed a variety of mental problems, ranging from anxiety and apathy to poor judgment. The remaining patients experienced difficulties in concentrating or remembering, speaking clearly, and distinguishing fact from fantasy. A twenty-four-year-old man believed that he was the first member of a new super race; another young man decided that he was a Ku Klux Klan leader who had been placed in charge of the Mafia. The report contained a variety of individual horror stories, often relating the experiences of good students who dropped out of school activities and became disoriented and depressed. Predictably, one of the students, concerned over his depressed mental state, was reassured that marijuana was harmless, by his college counselor. Dr. Kolansky called pot smoking "chemical Russian roulette." Young men and women who were psychotic were able to abandon their delusions after refraining from smoking marijuana, but lapses of memory continued to be a problem.

Even if we accept the suggestion that marijuana would not adversely affect the mind of a man or woman who is totally without frustrations or emotions, such individuals could exist only in textbooks, not in the real world. Even if use of marijuana does not directly lead to the use of heroin or LSD, a society which encourages (or even sanctifies) dependence upon *cannabis* is opening the door for further abuses. As James Burnham, editor of

National Review, has written, "We do know that frequent use of marijuana is often one element, and chronologically an early element, in the syndrome that includes, chronologically later, the use of hard drugs, though it is also true that in many cases the use of marijuana is not correlated with the later use of hard drugs. Whether pot tends to 'open the door' to hard drugs is an exceedingly difficult scientific problem, but the correlation is frequent enough to bring up a legitimate qualm or two to parents watching a child take up pot." As Jeffrey Hart, Professor of English at Dartmouth and author of *The American Dissent*, has wisely observed, the marijuana milieu can lead directly to heroin, even if marijuana itself does not do so directly.

Invariably, discussions about marijuana tend to overlook the positions of governments other than our own. The World Health Organization, composed of one hundred nations who cannot agree about anything else, disagree with the pot smokers. They unanimously voted (including the Middle Eastern nations whose culture has included an emphasis on drugs) to eradicate marijuana by 1985 and to classify it as a dangerous drug. The World Health Organization Expert Committee on Drug Dependence Position on Cannabis (marijuana) declared, "This Committee strongly reaffirms the opinions expressed in previous reports that *cannabis* is a drug of dependence producing public health and social problems, and that its control must be continued. While the marijuana issue has been turned into a holy crusade by many persons who depend on drugs as a means of escape, an even more disturbing element is the acquiescence of parents and teachers. Often, these persons have proven totally unable to recognize the element of peer-group pressure. Let us examine some leading scientific opinions on this subject relating both to marijuana, and the most harmful drugs like LSD. Dr. J. Thomas Ungerleider, founder of Project DARE (Drug Abuse Research and Education), retells the following episode: "I talked to a high-school principal who had forty kids who were stoned in school. He went to the parents. Thirty-six sets of parents told the principal to go to hell. Only four sets of parents came in."

Dr. Mitchell S. Rosenthal, Director of Phoenix House, observes, "There are dangers in the peer group situation. Adolescents are

very vulnerable to camaraderie, and the values of the group tend
to be infectious. If the group's way of dealing with anger at their
parents is to steal cars or use drugs, it is difficult for an individual
youngster to resist going along." Rosenthal goes on to advise the
parent of a young man who smokes marijuana, "His rationale, that
he and his friends and some of their parents see nothing wrong
with smoking marijuana, is a very thin veneer. If you don't let
yourself be bullied by this pseudo-sociologic bravado, you can get
him to think about the real reasons he is using grass. He will
discover that it isn't just to feel good or because it is exciting, but
because there are things he is worried about, that confuse him.
Smoking grass is not going to help that. It will only make him
continue to feel like a kid."

If parental irresponsibility is deadly when related to the
controversy regarding marijuana, it is deadlier when related to the
variety of pills that became fashionable for teenagers of the 1960's,
to LSD and the psychedelic drugs, and to heroin. Parents must
recognize that peer-group pressure is often very real to the
adolescent, and is still a factor on the college campus. Permissiveness regarding family life in general may lead to the assumption
that "It's all right to smoke pot." If pot is all right with dad, and
mom thinks that junior is just "doing his own thing," it may be all
right to try the stronger drugs when they are offered to him.

The difficulty stems from the fact that our society has chosen to
make the taking of drugs glamorous and fashionable, and portrays
tolerance of drugs as thoroughly chic.

While mature adults will gain nothing by merely expressing
outrage at the possibility of their children becoming drug addicts,
a greater danger exists. Often, in their enthusiasm to remain
"open-minded," they inadvertently encourage the cancerous
growth of the drug culture. First, they choose to ignore one of the
most important factors in the popularization of marijuana: peer-
group pressure. Dr. Fritz Redl, Distinguished Professor of Behavioral Sciences at Wayne State University and a specialist in dealing
with the emotional problems of youth, advocates the "peer-group"
theory.

He has indicated examples of youthful "friendships" in which
true personal relationships are virtually meaningless. Instead,

groups of individual young persons gathered, pursuing their own individual fantasy worlds, held together by a peculiar common bond: they avoided their parents and the police, introduced each other to drugs, and encouraged their drug dependence. Often the first samples of hard drugs would be for free, then for only a little money. Eventually, when the new friends were "hooked," they would be encouraged to earn their drugs by becoming pushers. The "friends" who persuaded them to adopt this course of action had in turn become pushers through the intervention of their own "friends."

Although Redl counsels against superficial condemnation of youthful drug addicts without an attempt to understand the reasons for their involvement with drugs, he also criticizes the opposite extreme.

He describes the attitudes of some teachers and parents: "Total surrender of clinical responsibility, frequently accompanied by a strange nostalgia for one's own (quite different) youth, or by a freakish over-identification with the young. Not only do the parents of brilliant kids fall into this trap, but I have witnessed highly competent youth-workers and clinicians regress to the incredible foolishness of thinking that the only way of getting rapport with the young is by imitating their hairstyles, their gestures and their dress so as to be considered 'in.'"

Redl goes on to recognize some startling reasons for teenage drug addiction. He continues, "For a large number of teenagers, addiction proneness flows from what I would term the handcuffs of the peer-group code. If we piece together the stories told by some of the rehabilitated kids, we learn that their first exposure to hard drugs occurred under the blackmail of this peer-group code. I refer not so much to the specific group of youngsters the kid went around with but to the image he carried of what his contemporaries considered 'a regular guy.' Some youngsters become overdependent on the concept of 'us young people,' usually represented by a fantasized character a few years older, several notches more sophisticated and many degrees less 'respectable' than anyone his parents would admit into their own basement without panic or rage."

Redl applies his criticism not only to parents, but to school administrators, teachers, and guidance counselors as well. In the process of accepting superficial or specious reasons for indulgence in marijuana, these men and women betray their trust and reveal their own lack of common sense.

Michael Aldrich, who divides his time between campaigning for the legalization of marijuana and Yippie politics, offers the hedonistic viewpoint: "Marijuana should be legalized because it's fun." Aldrich's viewpoint, despite its absurdity, is taken seriously by some who should know better.

Dr. Edward Bloomquist, an expert on marijuana, observes that "marijuana is fun" (in his estimation). He suggests that opponents of pot will achieve nothing by refusing to concede this fact. But he wisely goes on to observe that those who follow the Aldrich argument are choosing to ignore the numerous negative aspects of marijuana. Naturally, the fact that some persons consider an activity "fun" is hardly a reason for its legalization. Bloomquist, an articulate critic of the pot-is-fun viewpoint, has the answer. He declares, "One has to place the blame, not on youth who have the right to question and explore, but on those members of the Establishment who have the responsibility of presenting the truth. The tragedy is that some of our older citizens, entrusted with the education of youth, are mature only in chronology. Ideologically and ethically, these people are still adolescent. Through this immaturity, they find their link with youth."

Bloomquist cites the "expert testimony" of Dr. Joel Fort, widely recognized as an "authority" who regards the objections to marijuana as exaggerated. Fort, a sociologist, suggested that pot is unrelated to mental-health problems and not related in a causal way to advancement to hard drugs. Bloomquist, in detailed response, reminds us that his own clinical experience does not support these conclusions. He cites a study by *Psychology Today* which demonstrated a direct increase in tendency to use hard drugs in proportion to the likelihood of dependence upon marijuana. He also cites a bibliography of 1800 articles developed by the United Nations; although advocates of marijuana, lacking his clinical and medical experience, often claim no evidence exists that marijuana can be medically detrimental. Fritz Redl inquires, "Did you ever try to get thirty teenagers enthused about a

Shakespeare drama or a poem by Frost, while half of them are sitting around stoned or asleep?"

The point is well taken. We must beware of "experts" whose little knowledge of marijuana is indeed a dangerous thing.

Some observers believe that America's youth will establish the inevitability of legal sanction for drug activities. Already, high-school students are being urged to think in terms of "declaring their freedom" and "asserting their independence." The direction of this trend may be easily discerned; unfortunately, the path is not the magical road to discovery that some try to present. The Federal Bureau of Narcotics and Dangerous Drugs reports that the number of addicts *under thirteen* reported to authorities has grown thirty-two percent since 1967. This refers only to instances of addiction that have been reported.

Federal authorities speak of pre-teen addiction as being of potentially epidemic proportions. Newspaperman John T. Wheeler reports stories of horror and degradation directly related to the new drug culture. These are not theories or philosophies; they are not manifestations of the Establishment or middle-aged prejudice. They are the cold, hard, realistic facts that exist. The youth cult allegedly prides itself upon "honesty and reality." Apologists for the cult do not choose to be "honest" or "real" about pre-teen addiction. Wheeler discovered a thirteen-year-old Puerto Rican girl who had become a prostitute to keep herself in heroin. At Odyssey House, a New York drug clinic, he encountered a *seven-year-old boy* trying to achieve withdrawal from heroin. A fifteen-year-old Manhattan boy began taking marijuana at the age of ten, then turned to glue. When a friend of his died of a drug overdose, the children attended the funeral, in their own words, "freaked out on heroin." Wheeler related stories of pre-teen addiction from affluent suburbs and wealthy estates to ghettos. Teenage drug-taking occurs in public, on school buses, in full view of friends and neighbors. When advocates of the drug culture talk about the experiences which poor, unenlightened individuals have "missed," they do not choose to include a discussion of the permissive attitudes toward drugs which ultimately lead seven-year-old boys to heroin addiction.

Academic figures are not alone, however, in their general

approval of the drug culture. An example of this undesirable trend to permissiveness may be found in a recent broadcast of the network conversation program, "The Dick Cavett Show." Cavett announced plans to present a panel discussion on marijuana, with "all viewpoints" represented. In truth, only one spokesman was adamantly against the use of pot. Either Cavett or his producers invited an elderly district attorney from Texas to represent the anti-drug viewpoint. The choice was revealing. Certainly, we should not fail to heed the advice of law enforcement officers, simply because they are not young. But to present a program in which "all viewpoints" are purportedly represented, and to avoid inviting anyone representing a young anti-drug viewpoint is a manifestation of bias. This is especially clear when we remember that Southern law enforcement officials are identified by racial minorities with the civil rights incidents of the 1950's and 1960's. This in no way implies that the opposition of the district attorney should have been discounted, or that he did not represent himself well. But the attitude, which could be unconscious on the part of the producers or Cavett, is clear: opposition to marijuana is portrayed as "old," "Southern" (i.e., "racist" in the minds of some), and consequently "unsophisticated."

Representation of articulate members of the younger generation who oppose drugs would seem to be unthinkable. Apologists for the youth cult simply assume, *ipse dixit*, that the young viewpoint is only legitimate if it is inclined favorably toward the drug mystique. Spiro Agnew has repeatedly expressed himself against pro-drug biases in the media. But the Vice-President is subjected to criticism by the press, using the same biases they employ when creating a favorable image for the drug culture. He has declared, "In a sense, all adult Americans, and particularly parents and teachers, must share in the blame for drug addiction among teenagers. We have been too indifferent. We have been too lazy. We have been too permissive." He also criticized some newspapers, magazines, and radio and television stations for "making the use of drugs compellingly attractive to their teenage audiences."

As the Vice-President observed, the media reach tens of millions of young persons. Record company executives naturally assured the National Commission on Marijuana and Drug Abuse that rock records were not related to drug addiction. Stanley Gortikov, representing the Recording Industry of America, and Joe Smith, President of Warner Brothers Records, were eager to disclaim responsibility. But they carefully avoid the glorification of rock stars who admittedly insert double entendres relating to drugs in their recordings, and depend on drugs constantly as a part of their life-style. These record company executives try to disclaim such responsibility, but when an industry spends millions of dollars glorifying performers who indulge in and proselytize the drug culture, we cannot assume that this is accidental. A more logical assumption is that the record executives don't care, so long as profits are realized. Marijuana is illegal in most countries; even where drug addiction is widespread, marijuana skid rows may be found, resembling alcoholic skid rows. An attorney on "The Dick Cavett Show" summarized the pro-drug view when he said, "In a few years, the kids will put us out to pasture." But Dr. Edward Bloomquist called marijuana "an unpredictable drug used by unpredictable people with unpredictable consequences." It is not difficult to discern which viewpoint leads and which viewpoint follows.

Some, as usual, turn to the *non sequitur* argument of alcohol. (Irresponsibility on the part of young men and women is justified by the observation that some of their parents are also irresponsible.) Two basic fallacies exist whenever the marijuana-alcohol discussion is used as an excuse to justify the former. First, as Dr. Victor H. Vogel, parole chief of the California Rehabilitation Center has observed, marijuana produces distortions in perception of time and space relations (while maintaining muscular coordination), and a greater degree of tendency toward addiction and susceptibility. Second, as Alcoholics Anonymous will be happy to confirm, alcoholism has not been a particularly desirable element in society. Six million alcoholics do not speak well for the argument that marijuana is no more harmful than alcohol. Finally, the California Rehabilitation Center has released evidence that an overwhelming number of heroin addicts turned to drugs through the use of marijuana.

Especially in light of the attitude of the President's Commission, we are told regularly that "young people who know that marijuana is comparatively harmless, but still illegal will doubt our credibility regarding more dangerous drugs." This assumption is based totally on the premise that critical objections to the use of pot are really invalid.

While "progressive" writers and social critics have dwelled consistently upon the aesthetics of the drug culture, with its claims of love and brotherhood, they overlook another significant factor: money. The manufacture of drugs with subsequent sale is highly profitable for criminals, who have no interest in the misery they cause. Dr. Timothy Leary has been recognized as one of the leading promoters of LSD as a "truth serum." Leary allegedly attained his popularity because of his charisma, and his ability to communicate with young people. Yet Glen Craig Lynd, a one-time admirer of Leary, testified before a California grand jury that Leary's followers, who organized a "church" called "The Brotherhood of Eternal Love," had been major suppliers of drugs. Lynd testified that the Brotherhood, which earned thousands of dollars selling LSD, paid $25,000 to the radical Weathermen organization to help their guru escape from the men's colony in San Luis Obispo. Lynd did not accuse Leary of smuggling drugs, but the activities of the Brotherhood seem clearly to have been oriented toward crime and profit, rather than peace and love. Lynd described drug salesmen who paid $20 a pound for hashish, selling it for $150 to $200 an ounce.

Even a brief look at the facts about LSD shatter the drug mystique, and Timothy Leary's ideas of "revealed truth."

LSD is a drug which, when enough was injected into a 7000-pound bull elephant, caused the elephant to suffer instant death of a laryngeal spasm (loss of muscular control).

LSD is a drug, which, according to Dr. Hans Zellweger, Professor of Pediatrics at the University of Iowa and former Chairman of the Pediatrics Department at the American University at Beirut, is capable of causing congenital birth defects equivalent to those caused by thalidomide.

LSD is a drug which is capable of causing chromosome breaks, which may be inherited by succeeding generations. (In other words, chromosome alterations caused by LSD may be inherited by the grandchildren of the "mod," "enlightened" LSD users.

Typical malformations include birth defects involving children who have no arms or legs, legs joined at the hip at odd angles, hands or feet with odd numbers of toes or fingers, and arms or legs in disproportionate size to each other.)

Dr. Howard D. Kurland of Northwestern University and Dr. Charles Yeager of Langley Porter Neuro-Psychiatric Institute of San Francisco reported LSD as the cause of "solid brain damage" after extensive testing of hippies who use LSD.

Dr. Walter Alvarez, formerly of the Mayo Clinic, has observed that sticking together of just three chromosomes can cause mental retardation and bodily defects, and that LSD is capable of inducing multiple misarrangements of chromosomes.

Dr. Edward Pinckney told Jess Stearn, regarding LSD, "It gives many hippies the excuse they apparently require to live the disgusting way they do, since the drugs obviously block out common sense and the proprieties." Pinckney emphasized that drugs were often used to cover the inadequacies of users.

Dr. Doris H. Milman, a Brooklyn pediatrics professor, had a five-year-old patient who accidentally swallowed a sugar cube saturated with LSD. Within twenty minutes, she became a raving psychotic; nine months later, brainwave tests indicated that her I.Q. had ceased its constant fluctuations. Jess Stearn also reports the case of a professor's wife who shared her husband's expressed interest in LSD. Following experimentation with the drug, she abandoned her husband to seek a romantic interlude with the hippie who had introduced her to the LSD. After the hippie absconded with her remaining financial resources, following a stay at Haight-Ashbury, she finally became a patient at a San Francisco mental clinic.

In May 1971, a rock group, the Grateful Dead, appeared at a small rock festival (1000 persons is considered small in a field which depends on mob psychology.) An announcement came over the public address system at San Francisco's Winterland Auditorium, advising persons to pass their cold drinks on to their neighbors seated to their left and right. The result? The audience received a mass introduction to LSD. Thirty persons were treated for hallucinatory problems at hospitals.

This was not an isolated instance. A doctor was a regular staff member at the Fillmore East; rock music and drug disasters traveled hand in hand.

The most famous exercise of mass indulgence in drugs was clearly the series of rock festivals which appeared to be making a significant impact upon the new youth culture. Names like Woodstock, Altamont, the Isle of Wight, and the "Celebration of Life" festival in Louisiana became household terms. Young men and women by the tens of thousands flocked to these festivals. Reich sings the praises of togetherness, emphasizing rock festivals, an example of what he calls "a community based on having their heads in the same place at the same time."

Was the Woodstock Nation, enveloped in a drug culture, really the Utopian paradise that its supporters would have us believe?

At Altamont, California, the Rolling Stones were protected by motorcycle gangs armed with chains and knives in order to maintain discipline among the "kids." The promoters of the festival at McCrea, Louisiana, hired a New Orleans motorcycle group which called itself the Galloping Gooses—armed with chains and shotguns—to maintain discipline.

Two members of the audience died from drug overdose. First-aid stations were set up to treat hundreds of others who had indulged in what the underground newspapers described as "every known hallucinatory brain popper," ultimately resulting in "bad trips."

In the muddy Louisiana field, members of the audience indulged in mass nude bathing. Reporter Fred Sparks observed, "During the sun-baked days, naked boys and girls frolicked in a nearby river or dozed, sprawled out on rocks like so many lizards." The *New York Times* declared "The sweltering heat made nudity almost essential," compelling William F. Buckley, Jr. to declare this "a finding that would surely raise the eyebrows of some of those who worked in the *New York Times* composing room."

Perhaps the ultimate mockery of the youth cult ideal of brotherhood came at the Goose Lake Rock Festival. Two hundred thousand youths parked their cars in lots named "Layolot," "Astralot," "Tripalot," and "Takealot"; they walked down streets that had been renamed "Kilo Road," "Freak Street," "Zonked Avenue," and "Do It Street" to the entrance. At the gates, each of the 200,000 paid a $15 admission fee; walking past uniformed guards carrying guns or clubs, these peace-loving individuals encountered a mobile unit of motorcyclists, an electrified fence, barbed wire, and a ten-foot brick wall. The security served to keep people inside the 390-acre private park; they came for three days of uninhibited sun, rock concerts, and drugs.

One member of the audience explained his fascination with the drug-rock experience. He confided his feelings to a rock magazine critic. "Like you feel you're in a concentration camp back in Germany," he said, peering through the barbed wire at the armed guards. He concluded, "Like it isn't really America."

Such festivals may be profitable for their promoters, but as collective experiences they may be only interpreted as a form of mutual masochism. The orgiastic mass indulgence in drugs is neither a source for amusement nor a source of pride. It is, rather, a reason to be frightened. Far from the popular image of a celebration of life, this type of activity is a well-policed, commercially exploited exercise in apathetic escapism; it breeds only violence and immorality, and may be politely described as a national disgrace.

Many critics applaud the dependence on drugs of the rock groups; however, they will not choose to comment on the following.

Brian Epstein, thirty-four-year-old creator of the Beatles, died of an overdose of sleeping pills.

Jimi Hendrix strangled on his own vomit after taking sleeping pills and died at the age of twenty-seven.

Janis Joplin died of an overdose of heroin at the age of twenty-seven in Los Angeles.

Brian Jones, at twenty-five the father of three illegitimate children (three separate mothers) drowned in a swimming pool after taking drugs.

Author Jess Stearn recounted the tale of a girl from the University of California at Berkeley campus who was devoted to marijuana, and promised to write a report praising LSD to challenge Stearn's own anti-drug views. Instead, she was treated at Bellevue after taking pills, slashing her wrists, and putting her head in an oven. Stearn declares, "Of course, it couldn't have been the LSD or pot, for at Berkeley and other institutions of higher learning around the country, they knew these were harmless drugs." Various drugs are offered to the public as a type of truth serum. Unfortunately, when the subject is the drug mystique, advocates of "progressive attitudes" display little concern for the truth.

V.
The Triumph of Slobbism

If any single element creates instant hostility between members of generations, it is appearance. When conservative Americans are asked what they dislike most about many teenagers or college-age students, almost inevitably someone will mention "long hair" or "far-out clothing" or "beards," or "dirt and filth." But gradually, many middle-aged adults began emulating the customs of these young men and women. Businessmen, afraid to appear old-fashioned, began letting their hair grow. Even a former President was photographed with long hair.

Similarly, fashions starting with the youth cult were rapidly absorbed into the mainstream of society. In the entertainment industry, where images are so important, the older celebrities began to imitate the younger ones. Since the newer actors and musicians were often products of the counterculture, the effect was inevitable. When the new trends in bizarre clothing and appearance were accepted by figures who are glamorized in the press, other middle-aged citizens joined the party. In some respects, the changes in fashion have been exactly that: an elaborate costume ball. But little time has been devoted to the rationale whereby these changes were accepted. If we go back to the origins of all these changes, we find some startling evidence. The new fashions do not limit their influence to clothing alone: they affect taste, manners, and more. They ultimately encourage a new phenomenon: slobbism.

The fashions of the national costume party are well known:

95

jeans, bell-bottoms, shirts decorated in psychedelic colors, tent dresses, etc. Ostensibly, they represent an expression of non-conformity. They are supposed to express the whole person.

As usual, the arguments that support this view are disguised under the label of egalitarianism. Expensive clothing, we are told, enforces social constraints. A rip in a man's suit or a missing button from a lady's jacket are social indiscretions. Therefore, members of the Establishment must constantly be thinking about their clothing for fear of being held in poor taste.

The new clothes, we are told, give the wearer the freedom to do anything he wants. He can read a book, participate in athletic events, gaze at the stars, or even sleep in the same clothes. Everyone is free to be himself, to non-conform, to do as he pleases.

The fallacies in this line of reasoning are obvious. To identify them, let us individually select several neat semantical games played by the advocates of the new fashions. They have designed a clever label with some neat and commercialized packaging: but underneath the wrapper, we find the youth cult, squealing with delight that it's not only all right to look or act like a slob, but it's socially chic and thoroughly intellectual.

The myth of universal function. We are told that clothing favored by the Establishment, suits, dresses, various types of formal attire, are all designed to reinforce role playing. The new clothes are supposed to be functional in nature, functional as all-purpose dress.

It is easy enough to whine about the difficulties entailed in the wearing of suits or dresses, coupled with enthusiastic descriptions of clothes that are equally appropriate for playing touch football or sleeping. But what is clearly missing in this line of reasoning is an awareness that life is essentially composed of disciplines. Life without discipline is not civilized: it is chaos.

This in no way implies that subjugation of one's creative or aesthetic impulses to the commercial dictates of a specific career or specific materialistic values is necessary. "Thou shalt not kill" represents a form of discipline, one to which most men subscribe. The Golden Rule represents a form of discipline. The advocates of slobbism present arguments that are riddled with the inability to distinguish between excessive disciplines (or unfair ones) and those disciplines which *are* necessary. They cannot perceive the difference between a society totally free of discipline and a society in which restrictions are an essential tool in the establishment of true freedom.

The myth of role-playing. Social observers regularly suggest that members of the Establishment wear different clothes for the office, for work, and for play, because they play different roles. Superficially, this may seem to be a discussion of fashion. In reality, it is a consideration of values. Life is made up of responsibilities and pleasures, of triumphs and tragedies, of moments dominated by joy, pain, laughter, and serious deliberation. Life cannot be painted in a single color.

Many young persons who use this justification fail to realize that a man who wears a suit to the office and blue jeans when he plays touch football (i.e., John F. Kennedy) is merely recognizing that man has many functions in life. They are not the same. The desire for universal sameness is deadly all the more, when one does not recognize its existence. Regular bathing or neat, meticulous forms of dress may be minor inconveniences. Yet the lobbyists for the newest fashions applaud forms of dress, which by their own definitions do not acknowledge that man's clothing (which expresses himself) is not necessarily appropriate for every occasion. If a man is getting married, according to this theory, he does not have to dress more formally at his wedding than he does for a game of touch football. If a woman is giving a concert, she does not have to dress more formally than if she is going camping. Nothing is more important than anything else.

We are all amused by persons who are conscious of purchasing the "best" clothes from the "best" stores. Discovery of a false sense of values is hardly the exclusive property of this generation. A great difference exists between the comical, status-seeking man or woman, who tries to emulate motion-picture stars or figures in society, dressing in poor taste in order to be socially fashionable, and the man or woman who believes that it's dandy to go to church in blue jeans because it's too much work to put on a suit. (We can hear the argument coming: Jesus Christ wore a beard; he preached the spirit of humility.) What these zealots blithely overlook in their attempt to sanctify the unwashed state is that the men and women who gathered to hear the Sermon on the Mount did indeed wear simple clothing; but they did not deliberately cultivate bizarre forms of dress as a means of defying convention or as an expression of a new conformity to the tastes of a group of professional non-conformists. A prime difference exists between the individual who is neat and clean, wearing the best clothing he can afford, and a slob. (Dirt has its place in life; the new arbiters of fashion pretend to dislike sameness, but they do not condemn the universal appeal of dirt.)

Instead we are expected to believe that the right to be filthy in all places is perfectly all right, perfectly apropos in any situation. If a man is going to engage in ditchdigging, certain clothes are appropriate. If he is going to be inaugurated as President of the United States, his dress, his attitude, his manner must be different from his attitude if he is about to dig a ditch. By applying this curious rationale, we may suddenly justify *any* behavior on the grounds that man should not be playing roles.

One need not be serious. Being serious isn't comfortable. One need not dress in a neat or clean manner. This isn't fun. One need not be reverent, diplomatic, rational, or courteous, if one finds these attitudes constraining. Similarly, the clothing that is appropriate for any action is appropriate for every action. We throw our standards out the window. We condemn the pursuit of social status, and embrace the pursuit of comfort. "Comfort," in this frame of reference, means that which is most easily achieved.

The myth of relevance. Slobbism is justified through the excuse of social protest. The slob will respond to criticism of his appearance with the observation, "Do you think poverty or pollution or war is in good taste?" Attention is then shifted away from this self-appointed social critic's inability to govern himself to his ability to govern the rest of the world.

Thus, the pursuit of the radical chic and the fashions of the youth cult lead to a new type of status: irreverence for the Establishment. Although the hippies of the 1960's seem to have disappeared, and the campus ruffians are regrouping on a less vocal level, their forms of dress and attitude toward the social graces is being adopted in American society by the best of families. Thus, it is unfashionable to go to a restaurant or hotel where it is necessary to dress up—this would require a loss of wholeness and self; a dishonest constraint would be placed upon the "now" generation. Significantly, the stores, shops, and restaurants of affluent Beverly Hills, California are filled with young men and women who enjoy the benefits of their parents' wealth while indulging in today's new freedom. Pinning the blame on the Establishment has become easier than pinning the tail on the proverbial donkey. The affluent liberals and their spoiled children can enjoy all the benefits of what money can buy; but by dressing like hobos they can register their anger at the way the Establishment mistreats the poor.

They do not explain why it is appropriate to be unkempt, dirty, or filthy most of the time. Jeans, we are told, express the individual. Bell-bottoms bring dance back into our lives, and they even help us take ourselves less seriously.

Oddly enough, the talk about new forms of dress is devoid of objectivity with regard to the true conformist nature of the youth cult. Frank Zappa, for instance, admits that long hair was a prerequisite for consideration by the record company executives. Society regards Zappa's outrageous appearance as an expression of non-conformity. They do not realize that non-conformity has become fashionable. The real Establishment prides itself on a liberal tolerance for the new mod, hip, where-it's-at variety of non-conformist. In other words, only non-conformists conform to the Establishment picture of contemporary fashion.

If rock music is popular, it is because promoters are selling rock music this season. If bell-bottoms (or psychedelic shirts) are "in," it is because immature persons from seventeen to seventy are trying to keep in step with the journalistic image of youth. *Women's Wear Daily* and *Cashbox* have nothing to do with social relevance.

The myth of social progress. The counterculture has been inclined to hail the conversion of short-haired, neatly dressed young men and women to long-haired, drug-using "freaks." It never mentions filth or dirt; it is difficult to find any sociological justification for dirt, even for those who are adept at leap-frogging important issues. Dirt is unpopular with most people who bathe, and a defense of dirt would undoubtedly prejudice persons who are receptive to the New Politics but still prefer to bathe. No one

stops for a moment to consider the almost gargantuan influence of
peer-group acceptance in the youth cult. Being accepted by one's
peer group has been made an accepted part of social education.
Children want to be popular with other children, just as their
parents want to be popular with other parents.

Long hair, inevitably uncombed or ungroomed, old jeans, and
other all too familiar styles are accepted by the large number of
persons who subscribe to the counterculture. Although the hippies
are no longer an influence, we have not yet realized that what was
called the underground culture of the 1960's will move into the
mainstream of our high schools in the 1970's. This horrifying
process has already started. The slob may not be found searching
for truth in Haight-Ashbury, but he is probably on the local
high-school campus. Conformity is conformity, whether to the
folkways of Madison Avenue or Haight-Ashbury! Visit your local
high-school and college campuses. You will see a large segment of
students, dressed absolutely alike. They are being individuals; they
are non-conforming.

Young Americans are counseled to "cultivate being outsiders,"
which may be achieved through clothes, speech mannerisms,
illegal activities, etc. One should set out, according to this brand of
nonsense, to "non-conform" to a specific set of behavioral
patterns, all the while conforming to another set. With this
delightful system, a young man can go to school, conform to all the
accepted teenage patterns, and simultaneously pat himself on the
back because he has escaped the antique social charade of
"role-playing." He is misleading no one except himself. The role of
"fool" is as old as man himself.

The new youth-culture revolutionaries insist that it is ideal to
cultivate the role of an outsider, but execrable to go to the office
wearing a business suit because this is status-seeking and role-
playing. A double standard is handy for such ideological hopscotch. Youth presumably identifies with minorities and "losers";
Bonnie and Clyde, two notorious bank robbers, were publicized as
young people's heroes (banks being part of the Establishment, you
recall). Advertising is only objectionable if used to sell products
which do not conform to the counterculture. If a Hollywood–New
York multibillion dollar film company wants to glamorize "losers,"

youth understands. A California student newspaper declared defiantly, "Let's tell the Administration that we are going to have a new dress code WHETHER THEY LIKE IT OR NOT!". This occurred on a high-school campus. At the same school, a girl wrote an editorial in a rage because a school official suggested that the girls be required to dress neatly. Even on the high-school campus, dress codes have the capability of being used as an excuse for militants' mobilization of school student bodies as tools of the youth cult radical revolution.

The myth of the new taste. Concurrent with the new forms of dress, we witness the demise of taste. In former times, the standards defining "taste" were sharply delineated. Today, however, value judgments vary from social group to social group. Context seems to be of prime importance.

The new taste does not bother with minor distinctions; it simply reverses traditional concepts of taste as a whole. We are fond of smiling at nineteenth-century costumes, at restrictions of behavior, and especially at the chivalrous acts which all men were expected to perform. Taste was regarded as a sense of fitness, of appropriateness. Behavior was influenced strongly by context, and refinement was regarded as a manifestation of society's sense of context.

Edmund Fuller, writing in the *Wall Street Journal,* has described the sudden fascination for "non-upper-class speech" in England, following the rise of the Beatles. Fuller suggests that the reversal of standards, in which lower-class speech and mannerisms are imitated by those above them, is a sign of cultural decay and moral decline. He observes, "Changing tastes in art and manner interact. The effect is not one way but reciprocal. It is commonly argued that art does not influence behavior: Nobody was ever corrupted by a book." But Dostoevsky insisted, correctly, that ideas have consequences.

Edmund Fuller's point is well taken. The artistic manifestations of the new youth culture are often blatantly vulgar and tasteless. He goes on to declare, "The vulgarizing of speech and manners in much current fiction, film, and drama, lends an air of acceptability to the spreading indiscriminate coarsening of talk. It is absurd to suppose that the seeming acceptability of promiscuous sexual behavior and violence to which these arts expose us does not at least ease the practice of it to some who might otherwise hesitate. This interaction between art and behavior certainly is extensive on the lesser level we call taste and the profounder level we call morals."

Edmund Fuller has thus captured the essence of the youth cult: vulgarity and coarseness. Of course, semanticists try to assure us that all these terms are relative. By doing so, they deny that such a thing as good taste can exist. Rock record companies try to deny that rock music encourages drug use. But the dependence on drugs by the performers, and the saturation of rock lyrics with drug slogans, speaks to the contrary. Apologists for the youth cult assure us that dirty clothing or constant indulgence in profanity are merely expressions of "young honesty." But again, the evidence is to the contrary. If manners, speech patterns, and social behavior lose all sense of context, man's refinement, his degree of polish, the essence of his "civilization" are all gradually eroded. Duncan Williams has gone so far as to suggest that a society whose art, and literature in particular, glorifies depravity, cannot survive at all. In the place of man's refinement, we find what Fuller calls "aesthetic anarchy." We also find a massive effort to persuade us that taste is meaningless.

What we discover instead is a crude, vulgar, uncouth form of man, taking a giant step backward. As "college students, high-school students," and "the kids" learn to discard their upbringing and whatever sense of taste they have been taught, they embark upon a headlong flight toward slobbism.

Perhaps the most curious aspect of the youth culture is the basic assumption of a double standard. If a person is a member of the self-styled "now" generation, he may behave by one moral standard. If he is labeled, the "Establishment," he is expected to behave by another standard.

Any sense of morality is dispensed with entirely. Similarly, the intellectual processes which are used to determine such standards may be abandoned. We may reach conclusions by "knowing" or "feeling" and use these approaches to obliterate a dependence on reason.

"Reason" has had its detractors over the years, not the least of which have been the fundamentalists or ideological conservatives who place great emphasis on "faith." But as always, a distinction exists between faith or feeling and blind irrationality. A man who totally emphasizes cerebral processes may indeed become mechanized, unemotional, and motivated by attitudes that do not take into account human fallibility. But the opposite extreme, the man who reacts violently to society because of feelings or emotions may be in danger of falling into another old cliché: he may be saying, "I've already made up my mind. Stop trying to confuse me with the facts!"

One of the hallmarks of this procedure is the *a priori* assumption that a statement or idea held by self-styled dissenters may be valid by definition, the facts to the contrary notwithstanding.

We assume that some young men and women, because they have recognized the existence of certain flaws in mature society, possess a profound insight into the solutions to those flaws. Similarly, if criticisms are leveled at these proposed solutions, they are to be dismissed and ridiculed as old-fashioned and irrelevant to the contemporary age. Most of us can recognize that an earthquake or a flood is a disaster, but not everyone knows specifically what should be done to prevent these disasters from occurring, or to deal with them after they have occurred. This extends to social problems as well. We have fire departments because every citizen is not thoroughly qualified to put out a fire.

A brief examination of the inconsistencies in some of the statements used to support the assumption of "profound insight" on the part of young men and women who adhere to the drug-rock-bell-bottom syndrome quickly reveals the danger of ignoring facts.

We shall be on our guard for half-truths, conclusions not justified as drawn from premises, *non sequitur*, and enough varieties of inconsistent reasoning to make a tossed salad.

In the new taste, non-conformists are those who refuse to run with the pack. The advocates of the new taste are the conformists; they object to value judgments about their clothing, but do not refrain from using labels (i.e., pigs, Establishment, male chauvinist) to pigeonhole their critics. Their interest in the arts does not extend to the use of speech (or a mastery of the English language).

Instead, an inarticulate jargon, a private language, is substituted. Significantly, in the 1960's, the inability of teenagers to express themselves was a teenage phenomenon. In the 1970's, Madison Avenue has taken over, attempting to integrate the new non-speech into the cultural mainstream. Americans are being urged to realize, although they seldom do, that milk has something for every body, and that if you drink milk, you too can become as inarticulate as Mark Spitz.

Raymond Sokolov, writing in the *Saturday Review*, declares, "It's time for the new etiquette." Significantly, the new taste which started in the underground press of the 1960's has started becoming respectable. It is difficult to decide whether to take Sokolov seriously, because the new etiquette is so divorced from etiquette of any kind as to seem almost an exercise in satire. But his attitude, with or without tongue in cheek, is in many ways representative of the new perspectives. He says, "Everyone agrees that morals have changed a lot lately, that virgin brides went out of fashion in the late 1960's, that women are men, although less practiced at smoking cigars, that rags are chic, profanity honest, and old-fashioned good manners a relic of élitist deceit and of sexism from the past." The new principle of the new etiquette is declared to be non-intervention: in effect, the tasteful thing is to let advocates of the youth cult exercise their bad taste in public without being so tasteless as to raise the question of taste. (Parsing that sentence might pose a problem, but then again, "new speak" is here and grammar is part of the Establishment.) The new etiquette, captioned, "Buzz Off, Ms. Post!" speaks for itself. We are instructed not to assume that our unmarried friends of the opposite sex want to share the same bedroom without being so advised, not to be distressed by public nursing of babies by immodest mothers, never to expect dress codes, to be as filthy as possible in speech to all women between the ages of eighteen and forty, and wherever possible, to treat women as men.

At the Mad Tea Party, Alice learned about the un-birthday party; it was obviously invented by the youth cult.

VI.
What the Kids Want

The English language is constantly changing. New expressions arise every day. Yesterday's fashionable expressions are suddenly laughable clichés today, and today's relevance becomes tomorrow's memory. But one expression that is becoming a deplorable constant in the contemporary vocabulary is "the kids" or invariably, "what the kids want." Not the children. Not the young adults. Not young men and women—the kids.

In the heated discussions that erupt whenever adults converse on the whys and wherefores of young men and women, very few people bother to explain exactly who or what they consider "the kids" to be. Yet the media are constantly reporting public statements by eminent figures relating to "understanding what the kids want." Many persons assume that all "the kids" want the same things, or that certain self-proclaimed spokesmen are entitled to speak for the younger generation as a whole. Occasionally, a middle-aged adult professing to "understand the kids" will try to emulate those members of the younger generation of whom he approves.

Amid the confusion, it is necessary to remind ourselves of some basic facts about the younger generation. We must stop indulging in clichés about "the kids" or "what the kids want," and try to determine who, if any, are the true spokesmen for the younger generation.

Being "old" or "young" is relative; any adult may seem "old" to a small child, and even grandparents may seem "young" to a man who has attained his hundredth birthday. When mature adults speak about "the kids," many are not entirely sure which age group they are discussing. For example, when a recording company executive talks about "the kids," he may be discussing the nine-to-fourteen-year-old audience whose preferences dictate the stylistic direction of the multibillion dollar pop-music industry. When a university president refers to "the kids," he may be talking about post-adolescents or teenagers about to enter college. When a politician criticizes "the kids," he is undoubtedly thinking of political militants. Yet many of the self-proclaimed leaders of certain groups of political militants are curiously over thirty. By definition, one cannot expect the same tastes, desires, behavior, or social outlook from a nine-year-old who wants to buy the latest Beatle record and a thirty-five-year-old professional political militant who travels around the country trying to incite violent revolution. Many young persons fall chronologically between these two extremes. Most important of all, large numbers of young men and women do not adopt the attitudes or characteristics generally attributed to "the kids." These young men and women are often ignored because they do not conform to a preconceived notion of the younger generation developed by persons of middle-age.

Therefore, if any intelligent conclusions are to be drawn regarding the younger generation, it is necessary to first distinguish between various age groups in that generation, and to recognize the existence of individuals within those age groups. The younger generation can no more be divided into a neat group of categories than the older generation.

Because parents are responsible, to a great extent, for the perspectives their children develop, it is also advisable to take a long, hard look at the institution of parenthood today; we must try to determine why parents and children behave the way they do at this particular point in time.

Differences exist between juveniles, adolescents, and young adults. In considering the relationships between parents and children, we must remember the distinctions in behavior of juveniles, and their older counterparts who "drop out" of society, and those political activists who wish to control society while characterizing themselves as dropouts.

So much attention has been devoted to members of the younger generation that their parents have been neglected. The parents of the current generation provide the key that explains many of the dilemmas facing society today.

The current generation of teenagers was born in the 1950's. College students in their twenties were born after World War II. Their parents were in college (or in the armed services) during the late 1930's, 1940's, and 1950's.

Vivid memories of the depression affected many of these parents. Material security was of prime importance to men and women who had experienced varying aspects of the economic catastrophes of the 1930's, the recovery traumas of the 1940's, and the horrors of war. Simultaneously, parents desired to provide a better life for their children than the life they had experienced. Children growing up during the 1950's were not faced with wars or financial catastrophes. Americans recall the 1950's with nostalgia because these years seemed relatively free from trouble.

Of course, the post-war period was not free from problems; many of our present difficulties may be directly traced to conditions that existed during that period. Parents, trying to practice an "enlightened" attitude toward their children, depended heavily on progressive education and child psychology with regard to attitudes on discipline, authority, goals, and values. Ironically, the new economic boom of the 1950's encouraged these new attitudes. The children of the 1950's (gradually growing into the young rebels of the 1960's and the young men and women of the 1970's) were exposed, for the most part, to great prosperity. (The youth cult approaches the American economy as if it were composed of tycoons and manual laborers, with no socio-economic groups in between.)

Parents were eager to let their children enjoy the freedom from cares that suddenly seemed to be available as the war ended and depression memories receded. They were also intent on pursuing a variety of materialistic goals themselves to provide greater security and greater financial rewards.

In short, parents were enthusiastic in their pursuit of a world that would be totally opposite of the world they knew as children: A society dominated by depression and war.

Combining a desire for financial security with a variety of new psychological fads, parents became permissive as never before.

Donald Barr, Headmaster of the Dalton School and author of *Who Pushed Humpty Dumpty?*, has commented, "We offer very little resistance to our children. We tend to withhold reality from them by behaving as if there were no such notion as earning things . . . we think unthinkingly (so to speak) that 'yes' is a loving word and 'no' is a hostile word . . . Indulgence sometimes is, and is usually taken for, a lack of concern; better the father who roars than the father who shrugs."

Barr's point is well-taken. Parents were often busily pursuing their own financial security. (They were also seeking security for their children. But they saw this security in material terms.) Providing a "good life" meant a secure life; material security was stressed as an alternative to close family ties. These family obligations became less important, because father and mother were busy with other obligations.

Thus, parents, reluctant to accept parental responsibilities, maintained a pretense of family life while disregarding its basic tenets. The results were predicatably disastrous.

As parents confused love and affection with financial security, they also failed to distinguish between "love" and "permissiveness." This permissive attitude was aided and abetted by the emergence of a new "emancipated woman." Mother was not home when junior returned from school; she was pursuing a variety of careers or pleasures. Junior, of course, was enjoying a better life than his father had. When father was a small boy, he might have found his mother waiting at home for him when his school day ended. He might have faced some youthful responsibilities, because in the depression or post-depression years, a paper route or a summer job might have been essential as a means of helping the family. But such minor matters are of little concern to junior, since both 1950's parents were probably working.

The parents, of course, were blissfully ignorant of their folly. They were "giving" junior what he needed: anything his heart desired (in a material sense). Many parents justified their lack of real interest in their children by satisfying these material whims. From their standpoint, junior had "everything"; from his, he had a relationship with two persons who fell somewhere in between Santa Claus and the proverbial gift horse.

Many parents were hypocrites. Parents verbally stressed certain moral and social codes. Often, they advised, in effect, "Do as I say, not as I do." Father might insist that junior "Always tell the truth." But if father spends time boasting about his success cheating on his income tax, junior does not receive an emulative example.

Similarly, mother advised daughter about a strict and traditional moral code, especially with reference to marriage. But if mother indulged in a promiscuous affair with her husband's boss, daughter's adherence to a strict moral code regarding a premarital affair of her own should surprise no one.

Today, many parents are outraged if junior sneers at marriage, yet they themselves are often practitioners of infidelity. As a result, any teenager who knows how to spell "p-i-l-l" and thinks he or she has discovered some biological truths unknown to the rest of society may embark on a promiscuous life-style at a moment's notice. The old, out-dated moral codes of the 1950's become sources of amusement for the sly jokes among the pseudo-sophisticates of the 1970's. "Free love is nothing new," a confident teenager will declare today. "Our parents did the same thing, but they didn't talk about it. But we're different. We're honest. We tell it like it is."

Advocates of the "new morality" subscribe to this attitude, offering as an excuse the cliché that the young are suspicious of contracts, i.e., responsibilities that have been recorded. The point that advocates of the "new morality" miss totally is that in the promiscuous 1950's, mother and father were not adhering to the moral code they preached. This does not invalidate their moral code, which they chose to ignore. If many "mature" adult Americans have failed in marital relationships, the fact, in itself, does not justify the dismissal of marriage as an institution. Similarly, parents who pontificate about "honesty" while practicing "dishonesty" have not discredited the ideal of honesty; they have only emphasized the importance of an ideal to which they have failed to adhere, just as their children have failed. Junior cannot justify his behavior by saying that his parents are "wrong" about something. Possibly, both are wrong!

The basic principle is applicable in a variety of circumstances. If father tries to tell his son about the dangers of drugs, he will undoubtedly be reminded about any difficulties he has with alcohol. An alcoholic father does not represent justification for junior's becoming a drug addict. A promiscuous mother does not serve as an excuse for daughter to sneer at the institution of marriage. She may justifiably sneer at her mother's interpretation of marital fidelity. There is a difference.

Apologists for the youth cult are eager to beg the question. Whether or not father loses his equilibrium after the fifth martini has nothing to do with the medical facts about marijuana; such an assertion is irrelevant to the sensibility of drug addiction.

The father who does not overindulge himself can try to persuade junior to behave in an intelligent manner without negating his own advice through his own actions. Parents go to church and mouth the concepts of their religions: but do they practice what they preach?

An essential error in the thinking of apologists for the youth cult is the inability to distinguish between the failure of institutions and the failure of men to observe those institutions.

Parents seldom prepared children for the vicissitudes of life. Television represented a medium in which problems were finite and could be solved in thirty-minute or one-hour segments, with generous time for commercial advertisements. Children became accustomed to instantaneous solutions. In the real world, such solutions are not to be found. Young people find it difficult to reconcile the rules of behavior that they were expected to uphold as children with the realities of the adult world. Adults may choose to respond by observing that right and wrong are intrinsic values which are not negated by the confusion of the real world. This argument is only valid if the parents themselves adhere to the ideas of "right" and "wrong" they propose. If parents cannot live by the standards they impose on others, they fail as parents. Men and women who prepare their children to live in a world seen through rose-colored glasses have not prepared them at all.

Eventually, junior has a rude awakening. The children of the 1950's had their rude awakening when they found out that idealism is not easy in a world which regards profit, not principles, as a pragmatic solution to philosophical questions.

The dangers of instantaneous gratification and solutions may be seen in the manifestations of violence relating to youthful political activism. If junior wants something changed, he wants it changed now! He may not be interested in the way these changes may affect others. Problems facing society today are highly complex; they cannot be solved or eliminated through meaningless clichés or political slogans. Junior, of course, is accustomed to having matters handled his way, because at home his material needs have been gratified instantly. Unfortunately, society is full of persons who desire to maintain the status quo, and equally full of those who want to dispense with the status quo instantly, but have no idea what to offer in substitution. If changes are not made instantly, junior will throw a tantrum. Thus, a college is presented with a series of non-negotiable demands. (The demands junior makes at home are never negotiated; father and mother give him what he wants.) The demands may be immature, irrational, silly, or even impossible. But they must be gratified. If not, junior may be encouraged by outsiders (who are promoting their own interests,) to burn down the Student Union if the administration will reject the non-negotiable demands. (This is highly unlikely; university presidents are usually eager to agree to demands, because implicit in their agreement is the understanding that they are reasonable, rational men who believe, like the indulgent 1950's parents, that "Yes" and "No" are synonymous with love and hostility, respectively.)

Parents are surprised that junior is insistent on having his way—his instant solution to the ills of the world. Why? They have always gratified his whims. Can they legitimately blame him for being surprised that the rest of the world fails to do likewise?

Parents became followers, not leaders. A parent can hardly expect respect from a child if the *raison d'être* of his existence is the demonstration, through speech patterns, dress, and general life-style, that he has not lost his long vanished youth.

In their desire to be open-minded, parents are permissive. Most children possess an atavistic tendency toward mischief. But parents, eager to prove that they are not ogres, tossed discipline out the window. If five-year-old Johnny or six-year-old Mary breaks other children's toys or destroys property in school, we are told "Johnny and Mary are expressing themselves." When the children grow up and go to school, they will encounter professors who applaud their new disrespect for private property. The professors aren't telling the youngsters something they haven't known all along. The assertion that "people matter more than property" is a sterile cliché when used as an excuse for one man to take what belongs to someone else. Society possesses an overabundance of persons who want what someone else has. If every man fosters disrespect for another's property, he can have no complaint when someone desires to appropriate his property using the same rationale.

In later years, of course, if Johnny or Mary demonstrate a proclivity for irresponsible or criminal behavior, parents, quick to excuse themselves, wonder who is to blame. Johnny may have been an incipient menace to society as a child; Mary may have required some strong discipline at an early age. A parent who is afraid to teach his child respect, while filling his life with material comfort, is raising a spoiled malcontent; he should not be surprised that when junior decides to tell society where to go; he will include his parents in the invitation.

The juveniles who adopt the fashionable hairstyles, costumes, and speech patterns of their friends are not really indulging in profound social protest, any more than Huckleberry Finn was expressing sociological subtleties when he said "ain't." Children often adopt the patterns of speech around them, basic to their environment. If a child is not guided into a conscious observance of the precise function of words, he may become verbally inarticulate. (Is a long-haired, slovenly, eleven-year-old boy who says, "I'm what's happening," or "I'm where it's at!" expressing complex emotions? Hardly. He is merely conforming to the fads and fashions of his peers.)

Today's affluent neighborhoods may claim a plethora of boys and girls who emulate their thoroughly modern elders, the long haired, unwashed post-adolescents. Incredible as it may seem, certain self-styled mature adults are determined, at all costs, to regard these overindulged youngsters as polemicists for a new youth culture that must be emulated. (Most pre-teen children are inarticulate or grammatically careless because they don't study their English lessons carefully.) If these juveniles live at home, supported by their parents, attend school, and adopt only the superficial physical trappings of "hippies" or "now" generation college students, they are immature conformists; nothing more.

This same principle applies to high-school students who adopt these mannerisms. The process of social isolation which is generally described in the press as "dropping out" refers specifically to those young men and women who leave home and seek a new life-style. (The validity of this life-style may be surmised from previous statements relating to drugs, rock music, and the deliberate cultivation of slobbism as a panacea for personal inadequacy.)

An essential distinction may be drawn between political activism and total social abstinence. Both of these trends are essentially negative; a movement, deriving its basic tenets from that which it opposes rather than that which it supports, can achieve little. Many middle-aged persons try to "understand" the goals or positive aspects of these movements, and in the process, blithely ignore their weaknesses. To be sure, they pay lip service to a critical attitude toward the New Left, because they occasionally are willing to concede that political activism in behalf of left-wing extremism leads to a totalitarian society.

But they still act according to the assumption that the social perspectives shared by New Left political activists are justified. They fail to disclaim the irresponsibilities that permeate their behavior. The violent radicals cannot be dismissed with a slap on the wrist; it is a disservice to intelligent men to imply that the impact of New Left agitators or violent revolutionaries is seriously felt only by little old ladies in tennis shoes or retired generals living in Orange County, California.

In other words, one cannot dismiss the Abbie Hoffmans and Jerry Rubins, pretending that the New Left, once its revolution is complete, will suddenly become responsible and forget all those ideas about imposing a Marxist state on the people of this nation. It is absurd to say, "Of course it's wrong to burn down campus buildings," at the last moment, agreeing with many of the ideas expressed by the radicals, but side-stepping their inevitable efforts to seize power.

Sherman B. Chickering, editor-publisher of *The Moderator,* has suggested to us, "The activist is most likely to be the child of liberal Democratic parents; the hippie is most likely to be the child of conservative Republicans. The one considers his father a New Deal sellout, but adopts his father's Constitutional ideals; the other considers his father irrelevant, and rejects the prevailing culture entirely."

In considering the student activists, therefore, we are not talking about hippies or dropouts, but young men and women of college age, most of whom are still in school, registered for courses, ostensibly working toward the achievement of their degrees. (In student demonstrations, participants often have included non-students or street people, persons who wander on to the campus in an effort to exert their own nebulous influence. Student demonstrations have almost invariably been influenced or led by small handfuls of non-student leaders who travel from campus to campus, leaving a trail of chaos behind.)

The student activist, therefore, despite his dress, which may appear to be eccentric, or his methods of protest, is very much a part of society. Whether he should be a welcome part of society is another matter entirely. It behooves us to remember that activism in itself is hardly objectionable. What is reprehensible is irresponsible behavior that infringes upon the rights of others. The inability to distinguish between legitimate exercise of freedom and social or moral license is the great ideological weakness of apologists for the youth cult.

The first step in achieving a mature, intelligent perspective regarding the state of affairs on campus is the recognition that the academy may not quickly be divided into a neat, facile set of classified "heroes" and "villains." Many legitimate grievances *do* exist regarding the way universities are managed. As society placed greater and greater emphasis on a college degree, the value of that degree declined. The cycle continued to run its course with the subsequent devaluation of Master's and Ph.D. degrees. More and more students appeared in graduate school; as these advanced degrees became more ordinary, and holders of such credentials more numerous, tremendous pressures were placed on both students and faculty. The result of an environment on campus which encouraged the existence of institutions which were over-populated with persons who really didn't belong in college at all, was a great expansion.

It is difficult to determine any sense of logical or sensible growth on the part of academic institutions. Many of these schools are huge: massive, towering edifices, housing dozens of classrooms, crowded with persons of every size, shape, background, and with varying degrees of intelligence.

Much of the time a student spends in a university is devoted to procedures and processes which have little or nothing to do with education. A student is expected to assign many valuable hours to filling out reams of forms, paying heed to numerous pontifical procedures of protocol which do not make sense to anyone.

The university employees who receive the least amount of attention, an odd assortment of secretaries, teaching assistants, registrars, credit evaluators, and other persons whose precise functions remain a mystery to all, even themselves, cannot be ignored. (Lawrence Peter, educator, humorist, and creator of the "Peter Principle," calls them "professional automatons.") Often these people foster an obsessive concern for the keeping of records, the maintenance of files, and the evaluation of individual achievement against a cookie-cutter model which is capricious and arbitrary. University hirelings are prone to deferring to "the catalogue" or "the rules," although they are often unable to explain why there is any justification for these rules.

This attitude extends into the classroom. Ostensibly students attend a university for purposes of receiving an education. (Students often attend for other reasons. Husband hunting and political opportunism are as respectable as ever.) But many of the traditional means of evaluating a student's capabilities are anachronistic. The pupil is constantly tested or examined; the tests and examinations are usually less related to a student's ability to think or reason than to his capacity to participate in a social *pas de deux* with his instructors.

In large universities, the teacher may be a graduate student or teaching assistant, frustrated because the senior professors have free time to pursue their research or independent careers, while he must teach. In a typical general studies lecture course, the student may sit in a large classroom of fifty or a hundred young men and women, listening to a professor lecture for an hour. The teacher himself may be dull, disinterested, or bored. He may choose to read his lecture notes in a monotone, droning away while his charges glance wishfully at the clock, hoping that something exciting will occur to put them out of their misery. (This condition is not new; what makes it especially serious at present is that it continues to get worse, not improve.)

The student is expected to take notes during the lectures, and then memorize these notes, along with a lengthy textbook. Then the student attends his examinations, and is graded primarily on his capacity to parrot the lecture notes or facts extracted from the textbook. The professor may not possess the slightest inclination to discuss, to argue, or to inquire, all activities which are eminently respectable in the academic tradition. If the professor chooses a multiple-choice test, the grade may be assigned by a teaching assistant, or by a computer which corrects the student's papers. When this procedure is carried to its ultimate extreme, the professor is photographed reading his lecture notes while the students sit in another room watching their teacher on closed-circuit television.

The student may be expected to devote much of his time to courses or requirements which may have utterly nothing to do with his chosen career. If the student has not chosen a career, he may be using the classes in an effort to find himself; many young men and women are unsure of their goals or perspectives. They may need time and experience to reflect the ideas, goals, and values which may determine their future destinies. If a young man or woman comes to a university under the illusion that he will be encouraged to think, to analyze, to contribute, and to participate in a meaningful way, he is often exposed to a bitter disappointment. The elimination of outmoded procedures in the academy in no way implies a fostering of mediocrity or a debunking of excellence.

But if the student is expected to participate in an academic community which functions according to false values, not "knowledge" or "education" or "intellectual pursuit of excellence," but forms, catalogues, overcrowded classes, and arbitrary sets of rules, all of which serve to isolate the student in impersonal and dehumanizing ways, the student often responds in kind. (Emphasis must be placed on the word "arbitrary" when existing rules are criticized. Too often otherwise intelligent persons will imply that all "standards" or "rules" must be abandoned.)

If students knew more than their teachers (about specific subjects), they would have no business being students. A pupil does not instinctively know what curriculum is best for him; often we are exposed to ideas which may seem useless at the time, but valuable later in life. What is severely lacking in the colleges and universities is a capacity to slow down the machinery of the campus long enough to evaluate college procedures in a sane and sensible way.

Many firms make small fortunes selling pirated term papers to eager students who have proved willing customers. They sell term papers written by graduate students or teaching assistants who, for a fee, will do the research necessary to provide the students with term papers that are guaranteed to achieve passing grades. The educational process has become meaningless to these students. (The process is too widespread to conclude that only lazy students turn to these ready made papers.) The papers are, in reality, as relevant to education as the grades, computerized tests, and robot-like lectures. All are tools of artifice. If a student seriously tries to work for change, he is often told that the institution must proceed at its own lugubrious pace, capable of reforming only through the accession and consent of men whose self-perpetuation is directly opposite in instinct to reform. If a university (or any other institution) loses its capacity to change, grow, and evolve, it will ultimately sow the seeds of its own destruction.

All of this serves as a preference to the realization that the majority of student activists are not "reformers." A difference exists between reform (i.e., change for the better) and abolition (destruction). Author John Coyne has suggested that today's colleges are no places for reformers. Unfortunately, he is right.

The student who wishes to work for legitimate reform on campus is usually ignored. Instead, attention is diverted to the militant agitators who strive to take advantage of existing grievances on campus and turn these grievances to their own ends.

Ultimately, they are not concerned with the welfare of the students or the well-being of the campus. They are concerned with their own self-interest and the achievement of power. If some legitimate grievances may be used as a means for campus agitation, well and good. If not, they can easily create some grievances that may be used as a point of departure. Needless to say, they do not have to search very long or hard to find these existing grievances.

In evaluating the state of affairs in the schools, two unfortunate tendencies are easily discernible. One is the appalling tendency of some persons to deny the reality of legitimate weaknesses in the present ways of administering colleges and universities. (Strangely enough, persons who often quickly defend the present modicum of affairs in the multiversity have been "progressive" or "liberal." Men like Max Rafferty or Ronald Reagan, usually identified as conservatives, have publically urged a return to the "educational fundamentals" that seem so out of place in the vast university complex. But because sympathy for students is not considered part of these men's public images, their comments are usually ignored.)

The second tendency is the deliberate effort to ignore the existence of radicals who eschew personal responsibility in their own passionate pursuit of power.

This second tendency is exceptionally disturbing, because a man who loses his capacity for perception is incapable of evaluating anything, including individuals who may be sowing the seeds of his own destruction.

It is virtually impossible to discuss matters of student responsibility without immediately plunging headlong into an emotional dialogue which borders on the hysterical. A popular view, especially in certain highly influential academic circles, is that the whole concept of "student agitators" or "outside non-student anarchists" is more worthy of a *Terry and the Pirates* cartoon than the pysche of intelligent, thinking men. Academics often pride themselves on their abilities (real or imaginary) to reason. The professors are accustomed to functioning in their own little world; by nature, this world has been isolated, geographically and culturally from the mainstream of society. Professors also place great emphasis on the written and spoken word; faculty members are often evaluated professionally by the number of articles they have published in so-called "scholarly" journals. The fact that these articles are often exercises in trivia and competitions among men in pursuit of the ultimate in factual obscurity does not enter their minds.

As they place increasing emphasis on their own values, "meaningful communications," and the solving of problems through negotiations and rational discussion, they foster an inability to deal with elements who do not share these values.

If we are to escape drowning in a sea of rhetoric, we must make distinctions between the behavior of individual students or groups of students. When Spiro Agnew denounced instigators of youthful revolt as "an effete corps of impudent snobs," he immediately received a barrage of criticism from the press. Reporters and newsmen were furious because of the Vice President's seeming hostility toward "the kids," whose idealism and responsibility were presumed inviolate, by definition.

Similarly, when President Nixon remarked that he disapproved of the activities of certain students whom he characterized as "bums," the howls of protest were immediately predictable. No one bothered to consider the nature of the young men and women thus described. Instead, both the President and Vice President were publicly portrayed as unfeeling automatons who were out of touch with the hopes and desires of idealistic youth.

One is reminded of the behavior of demonstrators in Chicago at the time of the 1968 Democratic Convention, who armed themselves with an assortment of bags containing urine and other odoriferous forms of human waste. These were presumably intended to be dropped from windows of hotels, used to demonstrate the contempt of the followers of Abbie Hoffman for those who dared enter a Chicago hotel lobby expecting their rights to enjoy freedom from filth to be respected. At a Congressional hearing, one lawmaker inquired as to the seeming hostility of a policeman toward "the kids." The policeman, displaying a certain naïvete in regard to the minds of Congressmen, responded by demanding, "What would you do if someone threw a plastic bag of urine in your face?" Some Congressmen might honestly reply, "find out if he were a registered voter before offending him."

Doubtless there are numerous academics who would be quick to suggest, "In instances like this the desire for 'meaningful communicative protest' is being carried to extreme."

The absurdity of this attitude is obvious. Common sense should tell us that gutter level behavior is unrelated to serious expression of political protest. (To dignify such puerile, obscene acts is an insult to those persons of any ideological persuasion who engage in responsible expression of their views.)

Professors who cannot see distinctions between responsibility and irresponsibility have lost their capacity to exercise moral judgment. When they are eager to cry, "Right on, brother" to any nonsensical utterance or moronic exercise in demagoguery expounded by anyone who proclaims himself "anti-Establishment," they assume the stance and posture of the ostrich: their heads are firmly planted in the ground.

To return to the matter of rhetoric, it is easy to understand why the unwashed rabble of the Berkeley campus are offended by Spiro Agnew's references to "ideological eunuchs" and "effete corps of impudent snobs." When grown men reveal their sense of the inarticulate and advertise their ignorance by glorying in restroom graffiti, it is no wonder that the literate man, like the man who depends on reason, is clearly an enemy.

Generalizations are not enough, however, in criticizing the attitudes of such professors. Specifics are imperative, and unfortunately easy to find. A case in point is the People's Park controversy in Berkeley. This controversy stemmed from violence which erupted on the campus when university officials (and ultimately police) came into conflict with an assortment of students, non-students, and street people who wanted to appropriate a piece of university property, ostensibly to turn it into a People's Park. The episode represents, in microcosm, the basic differences between a normal society and the self-styled "People's Democracy" proposed by our self–appointed spokesmen.

Advocates of the People's Park refused to see the question in legal terms or within the frame of reference to private property. Ostensibly, these persons were proposing a new social order in which their particular ideas about ecology would be placed above the university's property rights. They claimed authority to make decisions not derived from the law, but merely from their own physical proximity to the land.

Apologists for the Berkeley street people are embarrassed by the suggestion that a society cannot function if a single element expects all other elements to do their bidding. On the surface, a group composed of students and non-students, encouraged by political militants, decided that a piece of property belonging to someone else should be turned into a park. Not just any park would be acceptable; rather, this had to be a park for the "people." But this term, "people" was always used interchangeably with the names of these various individuals themselves. The fact that the land belonged to persons who also could be considered "people," who didn't want the property used for what the militants called a "freak-out center," was unimportant.

Our society would be in a very sorry state indeed if a small group of men and women, even less bizarre than those at Berkeley, could proclaim themselves, without legal sanction, the "people," and set about appropriating the property of others for use by the "people." Explaining why anarchy doesn't work should be unnecessary in this day and age. But in Berkeley, society has often been turned upside-down. Let us re-examine the facts of the People's Park controversy and see exactly what happened.

One month after the university indicated its own plans to develop the land involved in the controversy, the local underground newspaper, the *Berkeley Barb,* invited readers to join in taking over the property, for purposes of making a park that would serve as "cultural, political, freak-out and rap center for the Western world." Immediately, a chorus of radical journalists joined in the fun, equating the struggle to take over the parcel of university property with such unrelated issues as the Vietnam War and ecology. (This venture into rhetoric does not disturb Reich, who only is upset by the use of polysyllables which offer an alternative to "the kids' " immature indulgence in obscenity.)

Ultimately, the Chancellor, Roger Heyns, and his personal representative, Earl Cheit, tried to establish negotiations with the groups of persons who began working on the property. (Naturally, well-meaning liberals, conservationists, and an assortment of local citizens participated as well.) The police erected a fence around the property when the university administration realized that the street people had no real representatives who could speak for all the persons involved in reclaiming the land, which had been littered with trash and debris before the efforts to turn the area into a People's Park began. Many of these well-meaning persons worked hand-in-hand with the militants who were seeking a confrontation all along. (A leaflet passed out on campus during this period suggested that the students destroy $5 million worth of university property if the administration attempted to reclaim the park land.) This appeal for blackmail with veiled threats of violence, is ignored by apologists for the youth cult.

When the police nailed up "No Trespassing" signs around the park, the Berkeley students and the ever-present street people took action. The allegedly leaderless students ignored the fact that the Chancellor had offered to develop part of the land as a park, while reclaiming the rest of the property for development as athletic fields and other similar purposes. Instead, the students and street people, following the lead of the student-body president-elect, who advised them, "Let's go down and take back the park," became involved in a mélee with police. The non-violent students and street people shouted obscenities as they threw rocks and bottles at the police. John Coyne has graphically described the details of this confrontation (and other crises of equal proportion on the Berkeley campus) in his book, *The Kumquat Statement: Anarchy in the Groves of Academe.*

Coyne recognizes the over-reactions (amid the chaos) of certain specific sheriff's deputies, while condemning the obvious invitation to violence by the anonymous, shadow-like leaders of the street people. Following the violence, the New Left Coalition drew up a plan calling for students to acquaint themselves with the use of guns, the study of Mao Tse-Tung's political philosophy, and adoption of a thirteen point program for revolution.

This program called for the turning of the schools into training grounds for revolution, destruction of the university unless it serves the people (i.e., the self-proclaimed leaders of the militants themselves, the appropriation of Telegraph Avenue and the South Campus as a haven for children leaving their parents, establishment of female communes, drug-distribution centers and marijuana cooperatives, the driving out of landlords and the seizure of their property, with the property rights turned over to the "people" (i.e., the self-proclaimed leaders again), establishment of Berkeley as a sanctuary for rebels, outcasts, and revolutionary fugitives, demands for forced contributions from Berkeley businessmen, abolition of police forces (with implied replacement by self-appointed vigilantes), experiments in communism, and relationships supporting the Black Panthers and creation of an International Liberation School in Berkeley as a training center for revolutionaries."

The most meaningful section of the program called for "Creation of a People's government," "not recognizing the authority of bureaucratic and unrepresentative local government, ignoring elections involving trivial issues and personalities." Also proposed was a referendum to dissolve the present government, replacing it with a decentralized government of neighborhood councils, workers councils, student unions and different subcultures.

Obviously, those persons, young and old, who sympathize with the "idealistic" young people of Berkeley do not realize that the well-meaning ecologists joined the vicious militants. The result was hardly idealistic.

Nor is this instance unique. Al Capp has asked, and justifiably so, "Does the *New York Times* think that, with this sort of encouragement, it will be long before New York Yippies take over Mr. Reston's car, while it is unused in the parking lot, and declare that a 'People's Pontiac,' or that they won't take over the unused cash in Mr. Sulzberger's wallet and declare that 'People's Bread?' "

Capp's point is well-taken. Mark Rudd has admitted that the "issues" which propel the militants are often imaginary or made up on the spur of the moment. Rudd declared, "We manufactured the issues. The Institute for Defense is nothing at Columbia. Just three professors. And the gym issue is bull. It doesn't mean anything to anybody. I had never been to the gym site before the demonstrations began. I didn't even know how to get there."

So much for the "idealism" of student protest at Columbia. John Coyne, in his thoughtful study, describes the Jerry Rubins and Abbie Hoffmans as "evil children." Perhaps this explanation is as good as any in providing some insight as to why they present such a clear and present danger to men of reason and goodwill. It is difficult to take Abbie Hoffman seriously. He appeared on network television with an American flag on his shirt, mugging and grimacing, sticking his tongue out at the audience, like a small child ready to demonstrate his arrival as an adolescent because he has learned an obscene gesture. Jerry Rubin charges $2000 a lecture, and travels around the country revealing the bitter truth about poverty in America. (Militant anarchists are no more reliable in their pursuit of wealth while representing themselves spokesmen for the poor and disenfranchised than hypocritical rock group leaders.)

Hoffman and Rubin would be funny, in a sick and pathetic way, if they were not possessed by the revolutionary spirit and had not the capacity to achieve adult evil in pursuit of their little boy quests for power. (Adolf Hitler must have seemed a buffoon to those who saw him as an Austrian housepainter with grandiose ambitions, prone to insane ravings about the ills that plagued Germany.) But Hitler's goals, his plans, were in his book, *Mein Kampf*, for all to see. No one took him seriously except his own followers. Too late, Germany and the rest of the world found out that an insane clown may become the scourge of humanity if he is permitted to achieve the power to execute his irrational, obscene, and inhuman desires. For this reason, for all their absurdity, the Hoffmans and Rubins cannot be ignored. Their goals are clear, as indicated by the revolutionary program adopted following the People's Park controversy. (Whether a People's Park or a Reichstag fire, the principle is the same.)

When well-meaning, but naïve men and women abandon common sense to talk about different forms of authority, they choose to ignore the obvious fact that in any society, order must come from somewhere or someone. The youthful revolutionaries capture public sympathy because they are glorified and glamorized in the press, Order as an alternative to chaos seems preferable, if man is to escape the law of the jungle.

VII.
Adolescence Begins at Forty

One of the most bizarre and fascinating aspects of the generation gap is the role played by adults who sympathize, ostensibly, with the younger generation. (In reality, they are expressing empathy with a selected segment of the younger generation.)

The nation has an abundance of persons, many of whom are prominent and influential to varying degrees, who are only too eager to express their enthusiasm for "the kids," and their concurrent disdain for the critics who express disapproval of youth's current fads and fashions.

The key to understanding these persons and their peculiar behavior lies in realization of the essence of middle-age. Barbara Fried, in her book, *The Middle Age Crisis*, suggests that the over-forty adult is not unlike the fourteen-year-old. He needs to prove himself. The middle-aged businessman is faced, for the first time in his life, with the prospect of competing against men who regard him as old, even if this term is absurd when applied to a man who is forty. Suddenly, he finds the role that has always been his usurped by others. The middle-aged mother may find her children growing up, with an apparent erosion of her usefulness. Her maternal instinct may be as great as ever, but its satisfaction may be sadly lacking. Both middle-aged parents may need reassurance that they are still attractive to members of the opposite sex.

One does not need a diploma in psychology to see that one alternative reaction to the crisis of middle-age is a resolution to prove one's self. Adolescents' awkwardness and lack of assurance have been the target of comedians and cartoonists for years. The fourteen-year-old boy may strut, swagger, and be predictably overzealous in efforts to publically demonstrate his masculinity. (He is not a man, of course, and when he tries to behave in a manner that he thinks is masculine, he succeeds only in becoming a caricature.)

When mature, he no longer has to boast that he is old enough to shave. Everyone else his age also shaves, and he has undoubtedly come to regard shaving as a daily chore which exemplifies no particular aura of masculine expression. A mature girl does not have to envelop herself in seventeen layers of cosmetics and lipsticks in order to appear "mature," as she may have tried to do when she was fourteen. She no longer needs to try to prove she is a "woman," because she is one.

At forty, however, the middle-aged man and woman have a good deal to prove. The trend has reversed. Instead of trying to prove they are mature (as teenagers wishing their childhoods were behind them), they want to identify with the young (in order to prove that their futures are ahead of them). The grass is always greener! We may sympathize with this dilemma, and even understand it. But the desire of a forty-year-old man to prove he is still twenty is not unlike the desire of a teenager to prove he is a man: in both instances, the artificiality of the masquerade dulls the senses, confuses one's values, and in a discussion of the generation gap, utterly unglues one's sense of equilibrium.

The "middle-aged adolescent," if we may assign that term, is easily recognized. In his speech, his choice of clothing, and most important of all, his expressed attitudes, he tries to emulate the young men and women that he identifies as "progressive." The teenage adolescent will boast about shaving, smoking, sex, and his disdain for traditions. Except for shaving, the middle-aged adolescent will boast about the same things.

In dealing with members of the younger generation, the over-forty adult may encounter boys and girls who do not flaunt their youth. The young man may wear a suit and tie, or favor short sideburns and neatly clipped hair. The girl may prefer dresses to pants, and even demonstrate an inclination toward hats, gloves, and a hairstyle that does not resemble a wind-blown scarecrow.

If these persons are college students, they are aware of their own youth. It is unnecessary for them to advertise what is obvious to them. Curiously enough, they do not regard themselves as stodgy, narrow-minded, or unsophisticated. But they do not deliberately dress or behave in a way which is identified as "youthful rebellion" by middle-aged persons. (In reality, these young men and women are non-conforming in the face of mass conformity which pervades the unwashed Woodstock society.)

If a bearded, sideburned young man in bell bottoms and a see-through shirt walks into the room, the middle-aged person identifies him erroneously as a "non-conformist." Simultaneously, this young man may challenge many of the values and ideas previously held by the over-forty adult.

An objective reaction to this person's appearance might be the assumption that he looks or behaves like a court jester (if he indeed behaves that way). This does not mean every young man who dresses according to the above description is a fool; it does not mean that he is a sage either.

The middle-aged adolescent, however, does not want to identify with anyone or anything which reinforces his own values, because he is basically insecure in his own personal and social role. He does not like the role of the "stuffed shirt," a role which the unwashed protagonist may be eager to assign to him. *He* is accustomed to being thought of as dynamic, progressive, and young. His over-forty instinct, therefore, is not to defend his own ideas or opinions, but to join in some way, the most glaring self-advertisement for youth and change. By joining the pack, he reinforces his own self-image as part of the youth movement gaining control rather than as part of the middle-aged society that seems to be destined for oblivion.

Perhaps the greatest source of his hostility is the conservative young man or woman. (Conservative is used here in a non-political context, with reference to a belief that change is not progress, necessarily.) The radical who wants to achieve sudden or abrupt changes finds a willing ally in the would-be twenty-year-old, wishing for all the world that he was not forty (or fifty). The middle-aged adolescent is scared and frightened that the world will pass him by. He is determined to prove to the young men demanding changes that he is one of them. He wants to say, "All right, I'm a reasonable fellow, I'm not like the other old fogies."

Fogy, a four-letter word, is perhaps the only obscenity left in the society of apologists for the youth cult. The over-forty man or woman is often tempted to discard his common sense, because the overpowering stimulus affecting his reason (and his relative security regarding sex and power, depending on whether one is a follower of Freud or Jung) is his desire to identify with youth. It behooves us to recognize that he does not identify with all youth; young men and women who may oppose violent upheavals in society do not reinforce his own youth image.

They are trying to preserve what may be constructive in our social and political systems. But they too are brushed aside by social and political revolutionaries who invoke their claims of "youthful idealism" as an excuse to advance their goals. The middle-aged adolescent, who could exert some intelligent influence, does not. Instead, he allows his fear to blind him. He is so desperately concerned about advertising his receptive attitude toward "change" and "progress," that he does not bother to ask himself if specific ideas or proposals really imply positive change, or even if the slogans or rhetoric employed by some members of the youth cult are really grounded in substance. He turns a hostile eye toward the young men and women who seem to be resisting these changes, even against the agitations of an assortment of groups who are part of their own generation. These young men and women are forgotten Americans. They are ignored by their contemporaries, whose very claim to legitimacy implies as a prerequisite their assertion that they represent all youth. They also receive the antipathy of the middle-aged adolescent, who regards any effort to identify him with resistance to change, even detrimental change, as a meretricious threat to his youth image. As we shall see in a moment, the error is fatal.

A relatively simple demonstration of this principle may be found merely by examining some instances in which middle-aged adults take curiously incongruous positions on controversies involving youth. We shall also see that these same middle–aged adolescents are perfectly willing to ignore or oppose the wishes or ideals of young people who do not reinforce their own youth image.

Consider, for a moment, the most obvious example of the

generation gap, dress. In various parts of the country, high-school principals have been besieged with requests to abolish dress codes, the rules that restrict clothing and grooming of students. In Beverly Hills, California, one of the nations most affluent school districts, the dress code was first repealed and then reinstated. No self-respecting college president or dean would dream of imposing any restrictions whatsoever on the dress or hairstyles of students.

The most curious aspect of this situation is the position of parents. Efforts by schools or academic administrators to impose restrictions on hair length or the more outrageous trends in juvenile fashion are often interpreted as efforts to impose the Establishment on the free spirit of youth. Max Rafferty, former Superintendent of Schools in California, now a university dean in Alabama, explains a teacher's point of view. He says, "Under the very best conditions, a teacher has his work cut out for him. Positively his hardest job each day is to get and to hold the attention of his restless, revved-up, captive audience. His competition of late is pretty stiff. In addition to the World Series, the Super Bowl, and the Miss Universe contest, it now includes discotheques, go-go girls . . . and *Laugh-In*, not necessarily in that order. Now, anything which makes it even a little tougher for the teacher to get his students to pay attention to him is bad for education. Period. So if your pride and joy ambles moronically into class wearing a beard or a Fu Manchu moustache done up in a snood, or a Mau Mau bone in his nose, for that matter, he's not just making an idiot of himself; he's also making it hard for his teacher to do his job." Rafferty goes on to counsel parents to avoid letting their children go to school dressed, for all practical purposes, in the guises of *Homo Neanderthalensis* in search of a cave. But Rafferty, always a controversial figure, because like Spiro Agnew, he does not pull his verbal punches, is accustomed to parental opposition in some circles. (Dozens of parents are distressed over their children's tendency toward slobbism. They are dismissed by the middle-age adolescents as "old-fashioned," or worse, "old fogies."

When teachers prepared to protest the obvious efforts of adolescents to emulate their assorted idols, usually the long haired unwashed variety, they were in for a surprise. Mini-skirted mothers, eager to reinforce their youth-image, heard the call to arms. Middle-aged fathers, often balding, with skin-tight shirts emphasizing their pot-bellies, but determined to sprout chin-length sideburns, were ready to do battle. High-school principals were not able to depend on their faculties however, because mini-skirted music teachers and male teachers with flared pants were hardly in a position to argue with parents.

Similarly, middle-aged principals were joining the bandwagon to the consternation of their superiors. The cycle, ludicrous as it may seem, was taking its toll. Why is this wrong? Doesn't this merely represent a change in fashion or a change in styles? Are these forms of dress and grooming merely offensive to little old ladies in tennis shoes, longing for the music of Lawrence Welk and the politics of McKinley? Not in the least!

The great weakness in the arguments advanced by Charles Reich and his followers regarding dress are doubly apparent when applied to parents and teachers.

Henry Malcolm has dubiously suggested that the bizarre dress styles represent an effort to "put on history." According to Reich, Confederate Army uniforms, or costumes which seem appropriate for the pirates of the Spanish Main (or the African jungle or the court of Louis XVI) are exactly that which they appear to be: costumes.

But Reich and Malcolm ignore the fact that wearing costumes is only a part of the new dress styles. Army officers were not dirty, filthy, or slovenly, and many of the people who wear such clothing today also fit this description. Wearing bizarre clothing is also a means of attracting attention for the person who has no identity in the real world and characterizes a fantasy world in which he can enjoy imaginary status. Abstinence from bathing is less a personal protest than a clear indication that junior is reverting to his primitive instincts. If he does imitate historical figures who were also guilty of slobbism, he is open to the same criticism as his idols.

When the parents and teachers follow suit, they are becoming followers, not leaders. A popular television commercial for a dishwashing detergent is a case in point. The commercial features a woman who squeals with glee to a somewhat befuddled looking acquaintance, while standing next to her own son, "I'm not his date—I'm his mother!" The implication is obvious. Madison Avenue is prepackaging a youth-image. If mother and father are busily trying to look like junior's dates, why should they be surprised when junior cultivates slobbism?

The motion picture and television industries are presently dominated by the world's largest army of middle-aged adolescents. Although studio personnel prefer to remain anonymous (they fear reprisals for even the most innocuous statement made about their superiors), the author has been advised constantly that studio executives prefer to emphasize hiring of employees who maintain a youth image. (This is indeed a pernicious form of discrimination.) One department head prefers employees who apply for their jobs in purple shirts, flared pants, and shoulder-length hair. Suits and ties are Establishment, and consequently, as obsolete as yesterday's cancelled checks.

The emphasis on the youth cult in the media is important because motion pictures, television, radio, and the advertising industries are responsible for the vast development of images and prejudices within the media. Dozens of public figures are trying to emulate the young in appearance. They fool no one. Senator John Tunney of California is known for his haircut which daily approximates an increasing resemblance to that of the Beatles. Senator George McGovern wears long, long sideburns. Public figures worry constantly about whether or not they are successfully projecting "youthful public images" on television. (This casts no reflection on the political views of these men, which is another matter entirely. It is true that conservative candidates tend to prefer more traditional forms of grooming, but politics is not the central issue. The question at hand is the effort of mature, middle-aged society to conform to the capricious whims of teenagers.) Charles Reich says that these adults do not succeed in fooling young persons by changing their appearance while clinging to obsolete ideas. But then Reich, a forty-two-year-old professor who wears long sideburns, proceeds to write an apologia for the youth cult. He fools no one either.

Often manifestations of the middle-aged pursuit of long-vanished youth can be amusing on a superficial level.

Consider the following, which was reported in *The Beverly Hills Independent*:

A resident of Beverly Hills told the city council that he caught a boy and girl having sexual intercourse in broad daylight on his front lawn. He resolved the problem by turning the sprinklers on. And to his consternation, the girl's mother telephoned him and bawled him out for getting her daughter wet.

The episode seems amusing, certainly with its comical aspects. But the greater issue is that this particular mother would not dream of criticizing her daughter's morals because this would seem "narrow," "conservative," or "old-fashioned."

If this pernicious tendency to model one's self after one's children, rather than expecting junior to follow the lead of his parents, can be a source of amusement, it is also a source of great concern. Consider the bleak implications of this phenomenon when applied to an explosive issue like racism. No better example exists than events that occurred at the University of California at Berkeley, when plans were announced to invite the convicted felon, Eldridge Cleaver, to teach a credit course in "Dehumanization and Regeneration of the American Social Order." Objections naturally came from the trustees and regents and in particular from Governor Ronald Reagan.

Cleaver, boasting a long criminal record, had served time in prison for selling marijuana. Upon weekends, following his release from prison, and by his own admission, he became a rapist. He was to pursue these acts until his subsequent conviction of "assault with intent to murder" which brought him a sentence of two to fourteen years in prison. Cleaver had often spoke in public of the desirability of killing white people, even including prominent public officials.

John Coyne, an eyewitness to the events at Berkeley, described the crowd that surrounded Cleaver when he appeared on campus, "Students, ex-students, non-students, dogs, New Leftists, hippies, street people, bums, Berkeley high schoolers, perverts, pickpockets, TV cameramen, lunatics, tourists, professors—the typical campus crowd—several thousand of them, filling Sproul Plaza from Bancroft Way to the Kumquat Grove, milled around waiting for Cleaver."

Ultimately, this same crowd attempted to hoot and shout down a faculty meeting trying to decide what to do about the efforts of the regents to invoke their authority and prevent Cleaver from joining the faculty. Coyne described the professors, as their "pipes puffed more fiercely, the tweedy shoulders squared, the faces flushed with pleasure, and the sidelong glances they threw at the crowd grew increasingly paternal." The professors, however, did not go far enough in their support of Cleaver to satisfy the mob, and when the meeting ended, the faculty members slunk home in the face of the crowd which stood by, screaming obscenities.

The image of college professors scurrying about in efforts to curry favor with an unruly mob is not a pleasant one. Why do these professors trip over their own feet in efforts to outdo one another in obsequious deference to a racist?

The image of these professors eager to please their student mobs is ironic; academics can exhibit the ferocity of a lioness protecting her young if a neatly dressed, polite, business-like student dares to question the most miniscule example of protocol involving approval of a term paper or thesis. Yet the same professors collectively will cower before a racist mob, all the while protesting their own "liberalism." These professors "understand" the young. More specifically, they know "what the kids want."

Racism is ugly. It is ugly anywhere at any time practiced by anyone—including blacks, a fact which seems to escape many of the middle-aged adolescents. In their desire to avoid being labeled "racists," many academics are willing to support racist ideas in reverse. Their excuse is a desire to demonstrate an open mind. If a mind is so open that it condones racism, it is exhibiting the openness of a sieve, not a well-functioning brain.

In recent months, certain "progressives," adolescents really, of both ages, have been demanding racial quotas. The idea calls for forced hiring of applicants for positions on the basis of race. (Discrimination against Caucasians is justified.)

Pamphlets distributed in Berkeley at the time of the Cleaver controversy urged that the university be blackmailed into hiring only "black–red–brown" men for positions on the staff. Qualifications were considered to be irrelevant.

Leonard Bernstein and his friends gave a now-notorious party in order to raise money for the Black Panthers. This party has been meticulously dissected by Tom Wolfe in his book, *Radical Chic*. (Wolfe, who was once highly regarded by critics who considered themselves "progressive," was quickly denounced for what was regarded as a heretical indiscretion: portraying the rich and famous lending their reputations to support black racism under the guise of liberalism.)

In San Francisco, the public schools prepared a quota system for the hiring of school teachers. Caucasians were to be given low priority ratings, with preferences in hiring devoted to blacks. This imposition of racial quotas is an obvious form of racism. But supporters of Cleaver and the Panthers cannot recognize the difference between an end to discrimination (i.e., equal opportunity under the law) and an effort to make race a condition of hiring. Hiring a man because he is black (or white, or red, or yellow) is similar to refusing to hire him because of his race. The middle-aged adolescents, eager to win the approval of their teenage children, are also eager to publicly advertise their guilt. This collective guilt, which they seek to impose on the rest of society, is supposed to be derivative of the terrible wrongs directed against the black people by our forefathers. In reality, it is their own weakness in combating black racism, as certain an evil in our society as the inane and vicious practices of the Ku Klux Klan ever were. Brotherhood is not achieved by racism, which comes in all shapes, colors, and sizes.

Particularly during this age of racial stress, it would be surprising if large numbers of whites did not feel an overpowering sense of guilt with regard to the treatment accorded the blacks. While in some ways, this reaction may be constructive in that we recognize past wrongs and attempt to right them, it can also cause problems. Guilt has never been the most desirable emotional stimulus to constructive action; this situation is no exception. If intelligent men and women suddenly become willing to accept any assertion made in the name of "racial progress," they become willing victims for those who seek not justice for the black man, but power for themselves.

In the French Revolution, the French people learned that true progress is not only triumph over a tyrant, but the assurance that one tyranny will not be replaced by another. Marie Antoinette was hardly a humanitarian, but neither were Robespierre or Napoleon. Today there are numerous "Napoleons" in all races, seeking to exploit racism to further their own ambition. Fortunately, in this country, legitimate means do exist to establish justice. These means may require more patience or perseverance, but they will ring true on a long-term basis. During the history of civilization, religious wars were common; although often fought in the name of "brotherhood," these conflicts caused only havoc. If religious leaders had truly practiced what they preached, the wars would never have been fought. Today, we cannot allow ourselves to accept demagoguery in the name of "racial justice," though the latter should remain our worthy goal.

Essential to this argument is the supposition that because large numbers of persons engage in a specific practice, that practice is necessarily desirable and, therefore, should be fostered and encouraged in the mainstream of society. Teachers have been encouraged to "understand" black English. Teachers, in other words, are urged to abandon their functions in developing and improving and instructing boys and girls in the fine points of English grammar. Instead, they are subjected to a barrage of criticism which demands that they function as auditors, who merely observe children and make no efforts to guide them in any specific direction.

If Johnny says "ain't," he needn't be encouraged to change his habit, because "ain't" is a popular term. If Johnny happens to be black, his poor grammar is suddenly sanctified as "an expression of black culture." Persons of every race and creed have a right to take pride in their own cultural development. These arguments may seem of little relevance to persons outside the teaching profession, especially when applied to the discipline of strict grammatical construction. By redefining concepts of obscenity, we only succeed in fostering the moral erosion which pervades a permissive society. If free use of obscenity (or portrayal of obscene acts in the entertainment media) is accepted as common practice, the resulting moral decay cannot be deemed extraordinary. Instead, we permit a gradual decline of standards without ever questioning why those standards have been established in the first place. Kenneth Clark, world renowned art critic, has defined "courtesy" as "the ritual by which men avoid hurting other people's feelings." Courtesy, along with polished speech and an emphasis on the social manifestation of manners, is the antithesis of the obscenity which permeates the youth cult. If courtesy and refinement are meaningful, it is because they possess intrinsic worth. They dignify man and expand his humanity in the process. A civilization cannot be expected to evolve (or change for the better) by fostering the ideal that no form of behavior is any better or worse than any other form of behavior. Egalitarianism cannot be carried to its furthest extreme without becoming authoritarian in itself. If obscenity is just as "right" or "proper" in society as any other form of self-expression, concurrently we may assume that other forms of self-expression are no better or worse for social progress than obscenity. To object to the self-perpetuation of any form of behavior becomes a form of restriction. But an absence of any restrictions leads to the assumption that morality (or the desirability of prevalence of some elements over others) is meaningless. If "right" or "wrong" become meaningless, man becomes concurrently amoral. He reverts to the law of the jungle.

In no way does the abandonment of a permissive or conciliatory attitude toward obscenity imply a subliminal yearning for censorship, abolition of free speech, or any other totalitarian practices. An unfortunate reality of modern-day society is in evidence when persons who denounce public obscenity are labeled "prudes." To accept the implication that any group of men or women regard the free and unrestricted use of obscenity as part of their culture is to merely encourage the most irresponsible and tiny minority of rabble rousers who seek to use "obscenity" as one additional means of advancing their own gains. If Johnny turns up in the classroom using four-letter words as an essential part of his vocabulary, he needs to learn in no uncertain terms the reasons why certain words are objectionable in polite society. It is high time that the middle-aged adolescents stop applauding the normalization of obscenity. It is also high time that we stop assigning "subtle meanings" and sociological implications to the pathetic utterances of those persons who best express their frustrations through the use of four-letter words. Teachers or parents who encourage little boys and girls to express themselves in the vocabularies of the gutter perform a massive disservice to society. Ultimately, these children will grow into uncouth primitives, only too ready to tell their teachers, parents, and the rest of society where to go. This will be accomplished in the basest of terms. Vulgarity is not "honesty." Crudity is not "self-expression." Obscenity is not "freedom." The middle-aged adolescent who cannot tell the difference is a sadly befuddled individual.

There have been voices in the wilderness, but too often these voices have been silenced by ridicule. Apologists for the youth cult dispose of their critics in a neat and thoroughly efficient way; they ignore them. If a critical voice is raised by someone who has yet to achieve a substantial identity in the academic or literary world (usually a young man or woman), the criticism is dismissed as immature prattle. (Apologists for the youth cult believe that young people should be "understood," but this courtesy does not extend to those young persons whose expression does not reinforce the apologists' own views.) If the objections are voiced by someone over thirty, he can be easily written off as an old-fashioned antiquarian whose stuffy prejudices prevent him from appreciating the subtleties of a Ringo Starr banging away on his drum, or the deep socio-political implications of John Lennon and Yoko Ono being photographed in the nude for a record jacket.

Grace and Fred M. Hechinger saw the handwriting on the wall in their remarkably perceptive book, *Teen-Age Tyranny.* Written during the early 1960's, the book deals primarily with the teenage society of the late 1950's and early 1960's, emphasizing aspects of the youth culture prior to the advent of hippies, mass drug addiction, the post-Beatle era of rock music, and widespread political militancy. But they recognized, even at this early date, that the mushrooming teenage culture was growing in an ill-advised way.

We know all too well where these trends have led. The Hechingers trace the beginnings of the problem to permissive parents and teachers. They comment, "The trouble started when all forms of self-expression were put on an equal level of importance and value. The child who just smeared paints across the pad was seen as expressing himself as usefully as the child who showed the beginnings of a sense of color and pattern." They go on to observe, "The youngster who had something original to say was given no more recognition than the classmate who merely babbled for the sake of the sound of his voice, or worse, his quickly recognized power to gain attention and disrupt the show. Ultimately, this view led to the extreme perversion of the progressive idea—the theory that ungrammatical idiom is just as good and as expressive of the real self as correct usage. In fact, there were some who began to deride the "correct" expression as society-dictated and therefore destructive of individual expression."

By now, of course, the idea that non-achievement merits the same rewards as achievement, coupled with the assertion that every manifestation of self-expression is "equal" has borne rotten fruit. Obscenity is glorified as "art," or "literature." Rock groups are assumed to possess profound insight regarding our social ills, equating their simplistic lyrics with philosophical wisdom (and musical expertise). Political violence is equated with "free speech." Immorality is justified as "doing your own thing." Because no one "judges" anyone else, moral behavior or artistic achievement are no longer entitled to the encouragement of society. Like all good theories, the concept of encouraging self-expression can be self-defeating when carried to its ultimate extreme. When someone criticizes this, he runs the risk of facing an angry army of critics, with pencils poised or tar and feathers ready, as the case may be. He is immediately accused of expressing desires for a return to the authoritarian form of education administered by a severe taskmaster who regularly exhibits compassion worthy of a composite Mr. Murdstone and Simon Legree. This is puerile nonsense.

If a child wants to race around the classroom destroying other people's property, he needs to be taught that this particular desire for self-expression violates someone else's rights. He must learn that the other children have rights too, including the right not to have their property destroyed. If students want to protest any policy of the government, they have peaceful and responsible means to do so. When they destroy property, throw rocks and bottles at policemen, or brutally intimidate other students who do not agree with them, they are not merely protesting, they are trampling on the rights of others. Apologists for the youth cult are willing to recognize the "right" of a student to break windows, but not the "right" of a man to live in a house without worrying about the possibility of rocks sailing through his window. They are quick to demand that all cultural expressions be received "equally." They deny, therefore, the right of recognition to a man who has devoted long and hard hours of work to his chosen discipline. If two men write music or author books or paint pictures, and one is exceptionally gifted, the gifted man deserves recognition.

To deny him recognition on the grounds that such a response discriminates against the less gifted is utter nonsense. All men are not created equal in talent or ability. "Equality" implies an equality of opportunity coupled with a recognition of the basic dignity and humanity that belongs to all men. But individuals do not possess the same capacities for achievement, any more than the validity of their moral standards or personal ideals is the same. The most dangerous aspect of middle-aged adolescence is the peculiar notion that society can function without any standards or morals.

Of course any attempt to impose standards or restrictions on any element in society will seem oppressive to those persons who are restricted. What the apologists and middle-aged adolescents fail to perceive is that granting equal worth to any idea or any achievement is to negate the processes of human thought that are essential to an ordered society. Charles Reich might be upset by the use of the word "ordered," because the use of the word is distorted by apologists for the youth cult to imply an Orwellian, totalitarian state. But a society with no standards or restrictions ultimately leads to a totalitarian state; concurrently it encourages dictatorship by a mob, and ultimately, by the mob's leaders.

Concerned adults must realize that by the time a child reaches college age, parents cannot suddenly expect him to develop into a responsible citizen. The permissive attitude must be altered or eschewed when he is still at an early age. What may be mild permissiveness toward the young child can degenerate into an obsequious "pals" policy toward the teenager and culminate in the spineless acquiescence of the middle-aged adolescents toward their young adult counterparts. The Hechingers criticize books, by authors like William C. Menninger, which offer advice to parents and teenagers, implying the family should be a "democratic unit," with junior encouraged to have an equal voice. They declare, "Having been pals rather than parents before, they now become a mixture of part-time providers, part-time social workers. But while adolescent hostilities do exist, of course, and should not be given exaggerated importance, the teenager who finds rudeness and disrespect accepted and explained away as a natural phenomenon merely revels in his victory over adult society. There are even strong indications that adolescents are testing their power at least as much as they are rebelling, and they fully expect and want to have a limit set for their actions."

Similarly, Dr. Harriett B. Randall, psychiatrist with the Pasadena Child Guidance Clinic and former medical director for the Los Angeles City School district, advises us, "Giving a child things, but denying him yourself may result in not giving him appropriate controls, or guidance. Substituting things for love, or thinking that things will represent love, fellowship, and contact, is a great mistake." Dr. Randall also says that children want leaders who offer protection, stability and guidance. She says that children do not want parents who are "pals."

Of course, young adults are not children. But middle–aged adolescents, seeking reassurance from the young adults that the forty-year-old imitators of the youth cult are "pals," check their common sense at the door.

Perhaps the most glaring discrepancy in the illogic that governs the theories advanced in the *Greening of America* is the inability to recognize the lack of constructive alternatives in the youth culture. K. Ross Toole, Professor of History at the University of Montana, has denounced the "tyranny of spoiled brats" and what he terms the "pusillanimous capitulation" to a small minority in the younger generation. Toole continues, "By virtue of what right, by what accomplishment should teenagers wet behind the ears and utterly without the benefit of having lived long enough to have either judgment or wisdom become the sages of our time?" He goes on to declare, "Common courtesy and a regard for the opinions of others are not merely decoration on the pie crust of society—they are the heart of the pie. Too many 'youngsters' are egocentric boors. They will not listen and discuss; they will only shout down and throw rocks. Society has classically ostracized arrogance without the backing of demonstrable accomplishment."

In this context, Toole is functioning as an unofficial spokesman for a sizeable community of middle-aged adults. He made these statements because he believes, with considerable justification, that the parental generation has abdicated its responsibilities of leadership. The "older generation," as it is often euphemistically described, has indeed come to grips with some of the great problems that plague civilization: Poverty, racism, war, and disease. Great scientific advances and medical discoveries have provided new hope for millions. Thousands of middle-aged persons possess the same desires for peace, prosperity, and universal goodwill that ostensibly emanate from the youth culture.

Poet Karl Shapiro expressed a concurring viewpoint when he said, "The American adulation of the child mentality leads to an industrialized hedonism on one hand, and a chauvinistic psychology of greed on the other. In advertising, anyone over the age of twenty-one or twenty-five is portrayed as an idiot who has got behind in the science and commerce of rejuvenation."

The "older generation" suffers from an abundance of individuals who seek to wear their guilt on their sleeves, eager to advertise their "responsibility" for all the ills of the world. War, racism, and poverty are complex problems. They were not invented by the previous generation, any more than a desire for solutions to these problems was created by the present generation. Ironically, too many young persons (and their middle-aged adolescent apologists) are willing to condemn *en masse* an entire generation of mature adults while failing to recognize the individual failings of their own contemporaries.

Toole advises parents to back the vast majority of young men and women who do not require apology. He admits, however, that this procedure is "too direct for those who seek to employ Freudian analysis, too positive for 'academic senates' who long for philosophical debate, and too prosaic for those who seek orgiastic condemnation."

Most apologists for the youth cult are quick to advertise the mistakes of their own generation. Indeed, the parents of today's young men and women have made countless errors, like all generations. They are also far more capable of recognizing these errors than previous generations. Nothing presents a greater example of the inconsistency of middle-aged adolescents than their ability to denounce the "mistakes" of their own generation, while failing to even recognize the existence of these same "mistakes" in the generation they defend. (In truth, they defend only a vocal minority within this generation.)

They condemn "racism," but they are silent in the face of the insidious racism of Cleaver and his cohorts. They condemn "hypocrisy," but they are only too eager to applaud the inane "musicianship" of prepackaged, commercially created rock groups so long as these groups echo their own political sentiments. They ridicule "conformity," but only if the term applies to dress, grooming, and speech patterns which differ from their own. Conformity to the folkways and mores of the youth cult is not only expected, it is demanded. They preach "love," but regard common courtesy as an institution worthy only of ridicule. They abhor "police brutality," but look the other way if the instigator of violence is found within their own ranks. They denounce "pollution," but are only too willing to support pollution of the mind through a poisonous dependence on drugs. They identify with "nature" but wallow in filth and squalor as a means of "social protest." They embrace "toleration," but refuse to tolerate any departure from their own myths and prejudices. They demand the right to be treated as individuals, but dismiss an entire generation with the cliché, "Never trust anyone over thirty." They express contempt for money, but are willing to live off the earnings of others, and to deify members of their own generation who achieve commercial success. They criticize "middle-class morality," but offer no alternatives save an epidemic of teenage promiscuity. They scorn discipline, responsibility, and tradition. Instead, they offer hedonism, permissive belligerence, and a bellicose disrespect for the qualities which render man a civilized being.

What is the answer to these middle-aged adolescents as they offer the unwashed minority their eager approbation? The answer is not new. It is neither surprising nor innovative. The answer is a return to the principles, a departure from which has been responsible for the current condition.

Adults must stop saying, "Me, too." Children are not leaders, although they can exhibit qualities of leadership. When they do, they should be encouraged to apply those qualities in constructive ways; not because, as Charles Reich would have it, society "knows what is best"; not because one element of society seeks to impose its will on another; rather, because human behavior has intrinsic worth or lack of worth. College students are not children. They are young men and women, and should behave in responsible ways. "Responsible" does not mean that they should abandon ideals or accept compromises with their desires, if they have them, to improve the world. The world can do very nicely with some persons who want to make the world a better place to live. "Responsible" means that one does not tread on the rights of others or tear down the foundations of Western civilization and American society offering nothing but mindless anarchy or aimless chaos in return. Families are not democracies in which junior's bedtime or his right to use the family car is put to a vote. This does not mean that parents should refuse to communicate with their children, or that one generation should be immune from criticism by the other. But "communication" does not imply acquiescence, and criticism is not a process whereby one generation appeases the whims and caprices of a vocal element of the other, for purposes of reinforcing its own youth image.

It is high time adults stop worrying about recapturing their own lost youth and start behaving like mature, sensible people. If the younger generation wants to abolish poverty, racism, war, and disease, they will find many welcome allies in persons of all ages. Perhaps, however, remembering some old (and still valid) references to persons in glass houses, vocal advocates of the youth cult and their middle-aged apologists would do well to start within their own ranks.

Consider the ramifications of constructive action. Otis Carney was a successful Beverly Hills television writer who had a wife, three sons, professional esteem, and considerable affluence. At the age of forty-six, he began seeking a "new lease on life" when he moved his family to a cattle ranch in Wyoming. The Carneys began adapting to their new lives as ranchers.

Carney was in a position to purchase a ranch, but even a large cattle spread represented a considerable departure from the life the family had previously known. Carney re-examined his own priorities. He decided that the life he really wanted could be best obtained in another way. But his family approached the matter in a constructive way. He did not become a middle-aged hippie, a polemicist for the drug culture, or dress like a court jester and buy a one-way ticket to Berkeley. In his book, *New Lease on Life*, Otis Carney recounts the episode of a long-haired youth who arrived at the ranch with some friends, seeking work. The young men rebelled when asked to cut their hair, even though shoulder-length hair is distinctly inappropriate in rural Wyoming society. The boys decided to return East. But following a lecture by Mrs. Carney, one of the young men walked at least twenty miles returning to the ranch. The writer's wife had challenged the young men's assertion that they were only "kids" and did not find it necessary to accept responsibility. Although his companions went East, the young man went to work on the ranch, cut his hair, and did his job well. Otis Carney observed, "I don't know if we helped that boy, or set him back in his search for himself. But I do believe in a few weeks he grew toward manhood, simply because somebody had challenged him."

Apologists for the youth cult would be up in arms, of course, because Carney, according to their way of reasoning, should have grown shoulder-length hair himself. The purpose of this behavior would have been to demonstrate to the youths that the rancher understood "what the kids want." These middle-aged adolescents do not realize that the "kids" often don't know what they want.

If Otis Carney's position on this particular issue is an example of one basic reaction in microcosm, the other side of the coin is equally valid as a case in point. Larry Uttal, President of Bell Records, is more unhappy than a child who has been made to doubt the authenticity of Santa Claus. Larry Uttal understands his son, and he wants other parents to realize that they obviously don't understand theirs. "I think if a parent is really in a position where he cannot stand his youngster's musical taste, then he's in a position where, at least subconsciously, he cannot stand his youngster," he declares. Uttal, once an unsuccessful songwriter, determined that he would "understand" the music and lyrics that appealed to his teenage son. He read about the new teenage idols, copied their lyrics down on paper, and finally, like the man who learned to love Big Brother in *1984*, Larry Uttal appreciated rock. "If you turn off your child's culture, it's the same thing as turning off your child," he declares. If we apply this remarkable piece of psychological profundity, imagine the possibilities. Junior, let us say, may choose to enjoy pornographic films, hallucinogenic drugs, or an assortment of vices. (Junior is too sophisticated for baseball or a good novel.) Suddenly, the parent who "turns off his child's culture," is ruining his child's life. If junior wants to study depravity, how dare his parent refuse to "understand"? Depravity may seem to be a strong word, you say, melodramatic and overemotional. Consider for a moment the "cultural" posture of Ray Davies and Alice Cooper. Davies is an English rock musician who calls his group The Kinks. Davies has been known to empty a can of beer on the front row of fans in the audience. The fans ostensibly reach up for the beer as baseball fans reach for a fly ball. Rock columnist and apologist Robert Hilburn calls Davies "one of the most literate and valuable writers who ever put his mind to the business of rock 'n' roll." But Hilburn, who indicates quickly his own level of taste, admits that Davies is not as elaborate as Alice Cooper. A twenty-four-year-old, long-haired *man*, Cooper describes his group's achievements with glee. "We get our audiences so crazy. One night in Detroit there was a motorcycle gang that was so stoned! I have an inflated rabbit. As I threw it out into the crowd, I yelled, 'Kill it!' One of the motorcycle gang started stabbing it with a knife. The gang charged up on stage. Police were called, but the motorcycle gang scared the cops out. That is entertainment!" Cooper chops up baby dolls and stages a mock hanging of himself as part of his act, which emphasizes fright and violence as part of "the rock art form." Lest we conclude that the young man with the strange name is sadly lacking credentials for sanity, we are reminded that off stage Cooper devotes considerable time to his investments and financial profits, and to his country home in Connecticut. A minister's son, he keeps his real identity a secret: This is an example of what Larry Uttal wants us to "understand." He says, "Just appreciate your children, and their musical likes, and take time to understand why they like what they like. If they could put the new math on a record, they might conquer the world's fiscal problems."

Fortunately, Larry Uttal, Robert Hilburn, and persons of similar "insight" have been content to devote their full time to ruining the record industry. They have not started to turn their talents to the world's economic ills—yet!

This does not represent an implication that all "young ideas" are as banal as an Alice Cooper performance. But the inability to distinguish between sincere youthful idealism and the psychological insecurity of pampered, spoiled brats can be fatal. The middle-aged adolescent is typified by the parent who cannot see the Alice Cooper phenomenon as a form of sickness. Teenagers and post-adolescents, obviously tired of television or films, need new "thrills" or "kicks." This was not always so.

Arthur Prager, in his book about 1930's and 1940's, *Rascals at Large*, recalls, "Society was definitely not permissive, sexually or otherwise. Youthful activities were strictly supervised and controlled. Pleasure was rare and hard to find. This toughened us. We learned to find happiness in small inexpensive things."

Today's culture is neither small nor inexpensive. The parent whose sole motivation is to "understand" his child's "culture," which he assumes in advance to be meritorious, is in for a rude awakening. Certainly young people have legitimate concerns about war, pollution, peace, prosperity, poverty, and other important issues facing society.

Thousands of adults, despite publicity to the contrary, share these concerns. But to pervert and distort legitimate hopes and aspirations of some young people as an excuse to grant any manifestation of youth culture the mantle of respectability is unfair and ill-advised. Prager goes on to remember, "Whole families would gather on Sunday evenings to listen to a half-hour radio program. Sandlot baseball and football were a way of life. As I grew older, the anticipation of a kiss after a movie date could be a kind of delirium. A dollar book, or better still a free one from the library, meant hours of pleasurable excitement. A Saturday afternoon movie was Heaven." The children of his generation did not need Alice Cooper.

Today, adults who are eager to endow their children with the innocence of youth and the profundity or wisdom of maturity are often shocked to find that their offspring possess neither. This does not mean that children cannot see through certain manifestations of hypocrisy or that teenagers or young adults cannot have personal identities. But often the confusion of the youth culture results from their very lack of background and exposure to life. At its worst, the new culture results in Alice Coopers, in sick, confused efforts to find new thrills or kicks, all in the name of idealism. At its best, the new culture represents confusion. A columnist once recalled his children's amazement when they discovered a "new sound" on a Beatle record. The sound, which they had never heard before, was a string quartet. Young people need to be guided and directed. They should be introduced to the best music, literature, theater, and art. Parents should remember that their children need to follow their examples.

They are seeking, searching, often trying to find themselves and establish a personal identity for their lives. Too often such considerations become exercises in the abstract. Young men and women are seeking "communication" or "their real selves." In truth they are seeking guidance and leadership out of the wilderness. The world is a confusing and complex place; there is no guarantee that specific members of the older generation can provide the guidance and leadership required. Obviously some cannot manage their own lives, let alone assist anyone else in clarifying his own values. But guidance and leadership (which may be expected in some degree of mature adults) will not be achieved if the men and women of American society plunge into a headlong flight toward middle-aged adolescence. How can adults deal with problems or challenges with insight and perception if they are devoting their time to copying, imitating, and approving any fashion, fad, or idea that is labeled "young," regardless of its intrinsic worth?

Donald Barr has counseled parents to provide alternatives for young persons. He says, "Parents must pass judgment with casual ruthlessness. The answer to " 'But Cheryl is allowed to!' is 'Our family has higher standards than Cheryl's family.' "

He also urges parents to find manageable risks for their children, i.e., sailing, mountain-climbing, skiing, football, etc., when appropriate. The needs to achieve, to accomplish, to prove one's courage are very real.

Parents cannot just be "against" drugs; they must be "for" a way of life which does not require dependence on artificial kicks or chemically induced escapes. If a parent cannot think of valid alternatives to drugs, he has a problem, and should re-examine his own priorities. Similarly, intelligent criticism of insipid rock music or obscenity in underground newspapers is not enough. Professors must be prepared to demonstrate the artistic and cultural worth of the great masterpieces of Western civilization. (Reciting some monotonous facts or declaring that Beethoven was a genius is begging the question.) Adults must recognize that cultural commodities patronized by young adults are not in themselves progressive or constructive, merely because of their origins.

Parents who devote their lives exclusively to material profit cannot offer regimented pursuit of "success" as an alternative to the dubious joys of unwashed hippiedom. Men and women who regard their own moral standards as conveniently adjustable to their pragmatic desires cannot offer "idealized" morality as an alternative to their own hypocrisy. Men and women are human; they are not saints. But society often revels in hypocrisy. Charles Reich and the other apologists can recognize some of this hypocrisy. But they cannot recognize the utter amorality and cultural sterility of their own alternatives. The professor, the parent, or the mature adult who says, "Me too" has no alternatives. He has only a vacuum, and is in many ways as confused and insecure as the young men and women whose behavior he seeks to emulate.

VIII.
The Quest for Identity

A popular television commercial recently has been informing viewers all over the United States, "You know who you are." Lest anyone assume that this commercial provides deep psychological insights, we hasten to observe that moments later the viewer is told who he is, or rather who he is supposed to be, a customer for a particular brand of cigar.

In another commercial, a nasal, feline voice purrs, "You've come a long way, baby." Within moments, however, women viewers are assured that the long way they have come culminated in their "freedom" to purchase a specific brand of cigarettes, "thinner than the fat cigarettes men smoke." Since the recent restrictions on cigarette advertisements, this has been removed from the air.

If advertising techniques today are less than subtle, they do reflect some of the problems that are on people's minds. Advertisers try to persuade listeners and viewers that their products are worth buying through the time-tested device of linking the product with ideas, personalities, or images that are deemed socially desirable. At one time, muscular athletes or military men and domestic, trimly dressed homemakers were considered to be suitable figures for public idealization. As new images are created and new personalities become more fashionable, advertisers adjust their techniques to a changing market.

Today great stress is placed upon the concept of "identity." During a period when enormous confusion exists as to men's goals, the hallmark of personal achievement has suddenly become, "knowing who you are." The implication, of course, is that the man (or woman) who "knows who he (or she) is" has discovered some essential "self" that wants to assert its identity, refusing to be intimidated or influenced by popular fads and fashions. Ironically, "knowing who you are," is employed, more often than not, as a slogan interjected as a means of selling commercial products for profit.

Unfortunately, the essence of identity is complex. Many men dislike complexity; the result is predictably an effort to oversimplify and indulge in truncated definitions and conclusions. If a man is asked to "identify" himself, his first instinct is to mention his name, to describe himself physically, and to indicate his profession, his family ties, and his background. (Rock groups are occasionally inclined to list their record sales before these other factors; actors may mention their agents in advance of everything else; the above, however, are applicable in most other instances.)

One of our essential social problems in the United States may be directly traced to the confusion that exists in the minds of adults in pursuit of their own goals. Men may develop senses of values in the abstract, but subjugate these values in the process of considering the daily crises that become part of their lives. An attorney who charges exorbitant fees or a doctor who cheats on Medicare reports does not consider himself "immoral." He rationalizes his wrongs by persuading himself that they are somehow "right."

The pressures of commercial careers may prove to be considerable. In politics, in the entertainment industry, in big business, and in large labor unions men are engaged in a hierarchy. An executive must worry about pleasing his superiors within the corporation and must satisfy his competitive instincts regarding rivals who may be interested in displacing him. This executive is on a constant treadmill; he must demand of himself the utmost concentration on efforts to reach the top. When he reaches the pinnacle of commercial success, he must worry about remaining there. Regardless of whether he is at the bottom of the pyramid or the top, he must consistently discipline himself to ensure his own survival. Security is virtually unknown. In fields of highly intense competition and enormous financial remuneration, these pressures may lead to paranoia, the abstinence from personal relationships, and the cultivation of man's basest emotions and instincts.

To compound the difficulties, individuals who become involved in such activities have little or no time to think, analyze, perceive, or reflect. Although the academic world tends not to be oriented toward the achievement of status or profit to the degree that business, political, legal, and medical professions are, the principle is the same.

Ultimately, such men lead pathetic lives. Outwardly, they are "successful." Let us imagine one such individual, and call him "Mr. A." Let us assume that Mr. A is middle-aged, married, with a family to support. Our Mr. A is an executive of an advertising agency. He gets up, eats breakfast, and hurries off to work. While eating breakfast, he worries about his problems, cultivates his neuroses, and dwells upon his anxieties. If Mr. A's children want to talk to him, he is too "busy." His preoccupation is with "important" problems. These matters concern his work. He rationalizes to himself that his devotion to his job is essentially in the interests of his family, because the money he earns can be used as a medium of exchange to purchase fine clothing, housing, an automobile, or even an education for his children. He estimates his relationship with his family in economic values rather than through human values.

At work, Mr. A spends further time succumbing to an assortment of pressures and anxieties. He may dislike his boss, but he flatters his superiors because he wants to "advance." (If he succeeds in winning a promotion, he is faced with the necessity of defending his job against an onslaught of competitive younger men who now hold the position he held previously.)

He may dislike his clients, but he must devote his creative energies to satisfying his clients' whim. If a client is displeased, Mr. A's salary or his status may be appropriately reduced. During lunch, he rushes through his meal, upsetting himself when he thinks about the afternoon schedule. By dinner, he is tired, irritable, ready to hurry home, only to be faced with commuter trains from New York to the suburbs, freeway traffic from Los Angeles to the San Fernando Valley, or a long drive from Washington, D.C. into the countryside of Maryland or Virginia. At home, his life does not improve. A variety of social relationships must be maintained, all for the advancement of his career. Mrs. A

wants to meet the "right" people and go to the "right" places. The
A's may not like classical music, but they patronize the opera.
Similarly, they may choose hobbies and leisure pastimes designed
to improve their social standing in the neighborhood. Golf at the
country club is infinitely more advantageous than woodcarving at
home, even though Mr. A may prefer woodcarving to trying for a
hole-in-one.

Mr. A has money, position, "success." He also has an ulcer, little
communication with his family, and little realization of the
purposes and goals of his existence. Mr. A has become the paradox
of our times: a successful failure.

Mr. A is a familiar character in American society. He turns up
on television, in the newspapers, and in the bestselling books.
Proponents of the new "mod" life-styles might even be inclined to
sympathize with the above description. Mr. and Mrs. A have a
problem. They are living their lives in a hurry; they are eager to go
"wherever they are going," but they do not have time to think
carefully and decide precisely where that place should be.

Let us go a step farther. Suppose Mr. A awakens one day and
decides that he wishes to radically alter his life-style. Imagine that
he quits his job, dresses up in dirty blue-jeans and a torn shirt,
grows a beard and shoulder-length hair, and begins learning a few
chords on a guitar. Consider Mr. A's friends; they will be amazed
and confused. They will complain that something is "wrong" with
their old acquaintance. He is suspected of being dishonest,
addle-pated, or eccentric for abandoning his "successful" life.
When asked what he is going to do with his life, Mr. A may reply
soberly, "I am going to contemplate my big toe!"

When asked about his family or their future, Mr. A replies,
"Responsibility is repression. I am no longer interested in conforming to the roles dictated for me by society." In turn, Mr. A may
subsequently go even farther and experiment with marijuana,
LSD, or other drugs. When Mr. A decides to wander around the
country "living each day doing his thing," his family and friends
will assume that the "real" Mr. A has disappeared. They feel that
he has lost his true identity. Psychologists who applaud the new
life-styles would disagree.

Mr. A has found his true "self," they would assure us. Inherent in this assumption would be a catalogue of the various hypocrisies and inconsistencies in Mr. A's former life. Herein lies their mistake. Even if we accept the fact that Mr. A's former life was devoid of many essential elements of human experience, does this necessarily imply that his new life is an improvement? Does it even mean that his new life is a good one? Does it prove that his new life possesses any redeeming qualities whatsoever? Of course not!

Mr. A's original problems stemmed directly from inclination to ignore his more humane instincts in favor of a series of artificial goals, primarily social or financial in nature. Because Mr. A made some errors in his first way of life, he has not automatically ensured the wisdom of his alternative life-style. If a doctor were to discover a vaccine that could cure the common cold, but this vaccine could simultaneously induce arteriosclerosis or cancer, it is doubtful that the drug would achieve widespread approval or popularity. If a man is plagued by termites, and exterminates them by burning down his house, he has achieved his primary goal but not in a satisfactory way. The sea captain who sinks his own ship to prevent some of the passengers from becoming seasick has, in the language of today's academics, "confused priorities." The list is endless; the point is obvious.

A man can easily become imprisoned in his role or its most obvious manifestation, his career. But to assume that any alternative form of behavior, regardless of the nature of that behavior is, in itself, a desirable improvement, is folly. To assume that because some disciplines are unwise, therefore all disciplines are unnecessary, is to provide not a solution but a replacement of one undesirable component with another undesirable component.

In the 1960's, one after another of our traditional institutions was challenged. For a while, "dropping out" seemed fashionable. Now, in the 1970's, with the passing of the hippies as a major social element, psychologists and sociologists are borrowing ideas and behavioral patterns from the counterculture. Gradually, the dress, music, books, speech patterns, manners (or lack of them), and ideas of the counterculture are offered to society as new influences on the cultural mainstream. These negative solutions to problems were not a panacea to the dropouts; when applied to family life or to the lives of those who have decided to drop back in, the result is predictable: a blueprint for disaster.

The basic assumption on which the new life-styles are advertised is simple enough: society places too many constraints upon the individual's "essential self." Man's real identity is lost amid his efforts to earn a living or to conform to society's demands. In the new life-styles, we are told, we can simply be ourselves, express our true identities, and forget about society and its evaluation of our essential selves. In short, "do your own thing!" On the surface, this seems like a basic plea for the right to non-conform, to be different, and to express one's self. Non-conformity is well within the American tradition, since the nation was founded by those who escaped the religious and political restrictions of their home governments by emigrating to the New World.

But advocates of the new life-styles do not really non-conform. Rather, they conform to a different set of standards, a separate group of restrictions and obligations. The young men who wear suits and ties do not conform to the fashion standards of the "now" generation; neither do the young women who do not choose to goose-step across campus by-ways or the local boulevard wearing military boots and practicing their women's liberation karate lessons. The young men and women who recognize weaknesses in the Marxist-collectivist collage of New Left politics run the risk of being ridiculed, of being called squares, or pigs, or worse. They will be ignored by a large segment of the "liberal" academic-critical fraternity, whose open minds do not include those who choose to non-conform to the doctrines of the "now" generation. Too often the middle-aged citizens who sympathize with the youth cult pontificate about non-conformity while eagerly awaiting the next trend or fashion which serves as a guideline for their own activities.

If any institution is slandered by the counterculture, it is the academy. Our schools are hardly perfect; their faults could fill volumes. Intelligent, constructive criticism of schools is both necessary and essential if our educational system is to grow and evolve. Ironically, much of the criticism heard today is not constructive. It often emanates from the pens of those self-styled students who devoted their student days not to study but to political machinations. Such critics often employ vivid and colorful imagery to portray the schools as prisons and the students as inmates. Then they use their premise as a theoretical springboard, not to propose constructive reforms, but to attack the whole idea of authority; invariably, their reforms call for power to be shifted from the faculty or administration to their own clique. Their demands usually call for the restoration of their "right" to do whatever they please in school.

Charles Reich was unhappy because the schools would not permit students to consider the option that, "America might be a bad country." Peter Marin observed, "The students I have worked with seem strongest and most alive when they are in the mountains of Mexico or the Oakland ghetto or out in the desert or simply hitchhiking or riding freights to see what's happening. They thrive on distance and motion." Jerry Farber's book, *The Student As Nigger*, contains the following passage, "School is where you let the dying society put its trip on you . . . our schools teach you by pushing you around, by stealing your will and your sense of power, by making timid, apathetic slaves of you . . . authority addicts."

Assuming that students are responsible and capable of assuming more authority, what alternatives are they offering to the present system? Some "students" at Columbia chanted, "Kill all adults" at a "peaceful" political rally. If the students are not encouraged to hitchike or ride freights to see what's happening for university credit, are they being turned into authority addicts? We must distinguish between the legitimate protest of individuals who wish to express themselves and immature, unstable men and women with the outlook of spoiled children, who want the world on their own ideological string.

During the 1960's, campus militants were demanding that the universities be reconstructed to consider the option that "America might be a bad country." Invariably, their search for truth led not to truth, but to the hopped-up, turned-on, glamorized stew of collectivism. Certainly the faculty of the University of California at Berkeley has demonstrated no particular sympathy for the "free speech" rights of faculty members who do not espouse the political views held by a majority of the faculty. Some students prefer to assume that in a Communism versus Democracy course, the objective professor can only present the sides "equally." If an *objective* presentation of the facts supports one viewpoint over its alternative, faculty members cannot be chastised for letting the students draw their own conclusions. It is inconceivable to some that *objectively*, democracy may be superior to communism, and therefore, receive the more favorable presentation in the classroom. The professor is not disturbed about the possibility of bias on the part of faculty members who may prefer communism to democracy. (Demonstrating his customary pro-left bias, he is distraught over a possible bias in favor of the freer forms of government, but not over the attitudes of Angela Davis, Herbert Marcuse, or other Marxists who teach.) The United States has a tradition of free speech and dissent not apparent in the classrooms where students are taught only the quotations of Chairman Mao. It is ironic that liberal opponents of any classroom indoctrination, have chosen to disparage the political system which is least encouraging to such procedures.

When the principle is carried to its ultimate extreme, the absurdity of these arguments is apparent. If a faculty member were to carry on a class discussion on the subject of Clean Air versus Pollution, would he lose his objectivity in making the former appear more desirable to the latter?

If such exercises in semantics may appear to be submerged in philosophical subtleties, no such enigmas restrict us in our evaluation of this principle as applied to the elementary and secondary levels of education. Mischief is older than Chaucer and as American as Mark Twain. Small boys have a natural bent toward engaging in activities that are inadvisable. Little girls, despite their more feminine restraints, have been known to exhibit the same tendencies. But suddenly, childish mischief possesses deep sociological implications. If a boy wants to dip a girl's hair in an inkwell, blow bubblegum bubbles during his arithmetic lesson, or place a box of thumbtacks on teacher's chair, he is expressing "his essential self." Efforts to discipline him are characterized as "indoctrination." When a critic is protesting the establishment of a society based upon "meritocracy," he refuses to accept as a syllogistic premise the proposition that some forms of behavior (or some ideas) possess more intrinsic merit than others.

We may easily recognize that a "meritocracy" may possess some drawbacks. In various roles or professions, the nature of "merit" may be determined by organizations or individuals who have acquired influence in a given field. The youth cult is outraged by the implication that "merit" is normally applied only in its functional sense, rather than in ways which are "aesthetically meaningful" to those who wish to turn society inside-out.

Unfortunately, society possesses no alternative to this perspective. If "merit," regardless of its definition, is not applied as a means for distinguishing between men, what other standard is equally valid? The assumption that financially remunerative professions mean that persons thereby engaged are "better" or "superior" than persons engaged in activities which provide little financial reward is unfortunate. Such attitudes will persist as long as man continues to evaluate other men in materialistic terms. If the popularly held notion that a lawyer is more "successful" than a bricklayer is undesirable, the condition will not improve because a third party intervenes with the intent of establishing financial parity between lawyers and bricklayers.

In the event that attempts at financial leveling are undertaken by the state, the ultimate result will not be the upgrading of bricklayers, but the downgrading of lawyers. Concurrently, the establishment of such "equality" is in fact the blatant sanction of *inequality*, and a significant step toward Big Brother.

To recognize that the highly specialized services of some physicians or attorneys are less easily obtained in society than the services of manual laborers is merely to acknowledge the demands of the marketplace. Efforts to control such demands have been historically disastrous.

In academic circumstances, teachers find it necessary to depend on a variety of grading procedures in evaluating students.

Initially, a prime function of "grading" was to inform the student of the nature of his work. In a teacher–pupil relationship, meaningful progress cannot be achieved if the pupil is presumed to know more about the subject studied than the instructor. In practice, grading has often degenerated into an artificial teaching tool that enables incompetent instructors to threaten or abuse students who do not share their beliefs. (This reference is primarily to forms of higher education. If a sixth grader chooses to believe that fractions are irrelevant to making change, or a fourth grader decides that $2 + 2 = 5$, we cannot speak of differences of opinion.)

Too often a grade becomes an artificial symbol; the student must pursue the grade, not the knowledge. In turn, the grade may be achieved by compliance with standards or techniques which are essentially unrelated to the discipline as a whole. Testing or examination procedures may be abusive or unfair. Multiple-choice tests present classic examples of a test form which, when applied arbitrarily, may penalize the thinking student in favor of his less imaginative colleagues.

But again, reason must prevail. Even if educators freely concede that grading and testing procedures need careful re-examination, such changes must be approached from the standpoint of reform if the system of education is to survive. If examinations for drivers who seek applications fail to eliminate all unsafe drivers, we should not therefore abolish the procedure of driver-testing.

Intelligent criticism may be directed at a variety of teaching techniques and procedures as means of evaluating student performance. But efforts to abolish "merit" as a *sine qua non* consideration in student–teacher relationships is to go far beyond the boundaries of intelligent criticism.

If a teacher or principal cannot set standards for merit, who should? Certainly, students themselves are not in a position to set such standards for their own self-interest precludes objectivity. Advocates of "student power" are willing to assume the corruptibility of private corporations and the inefficiency of the regulatory agencies responsible for overseeing their activities.

Why then must we fail to challenge the peculiar notion that the perfectability of man is applicable to high-school students but not corporation executives? Are teenagers more qualified to evaluate their own work than businessmen?

An unfortunate corollary in such discussions often interferes with an intelligent solution. Objections to the abolition of a "meritocracy" are dismissed as stubborn, unfeeling resistance to the inevitability of change. If specifics are examined, however, we easily see how the misinterpretation of faculty authority may be a stimulus to academic deterioration.

Students are often inclined to assume that their present tastes in books, films, music, and art are more *relevant* to their futures than time spent acquiring a familiarity with the cogent ideas and significant achievements of former times. A negative view of tradition is often encouraged by middle-aged professors nervously trying to identify with contemporary trends, thus preserving their own claims to professional esteem. Equation of "newness" with relevance is distinctly ill-advised. Wiley Housewright, former President of Music Educators' National Conference, urged that public schools begin immediately introducing rock music into their curricula. A basis for this proposition was Housewright's assumption that the music which was most familiar to young people would be a valuable teaching aid in "communicating" with them. Similar arguments could be advanced in behalf of such dubiously non-academic publications as comic books, *Mad* magazine, baseball cards, motion picture gossip magazines, and other items of interest to children. If a majority of sixth graders were invited to choose between spending an hour learning to read or watching television, the children might instinctively select the latter, even though the former would be infinitely more "relevant" to their education.

Similarly, ice cream cones are more "relevant" than spinach. Wiley Housewright was oblivious to the nature of teaching when he decided to jump on the bandwagon of teachers who feel that pop music communicates with children. If boys and girls are not already inundated to a point of saturation with commercially prepackaged pop culture, they will be when their "progressive" teachers are through with them.

Housewright assumed that because rock music exists, it is therefore "relevant." But the mere existence of any aspect, characteristic, or element in a culture does not in itself justify its inclusion in the curriculum. To suggest that students' judgment and teachers' judgment are collectively "equal" is nonsense. A hallmark of befuddled thinking with reference to the curriculum has arisen during the last few years. A number of educators have taken to suggesting that all subjects not deemed "relevant" by high-school or college students should be eliminated entirely from the curriculum. A further suggestion implies that faculty members who have insisted on the validity of these subjects should feel guilty regarding their past indiscretion. Profound exercises in public guilt are fashionable among apologists for the youth cult, who seem to regard a public confession of past aberrations in the name of tradition as an initiation exercise in progressive thought.

College catalogues are full of courses that are indeed irrelevant, unnecessary, and useless. The professor who turns his class over to an assistant, who drones and mumbles his fifteen-year-old lecture notes, and then assigns a devastating "grade" to his pupils, based on a single terrifying examination, is helping no one. But if the narrow-minded, trivia-seeking, incompetent bureaucrat is a vestigial participant in today's academic world, so is the self-appointed, egocentric, ignorant youth who regards his own immature whims as a suitable curriculum for himself and everyone else.

During one such controversy, a militant young man complained that because he was black, he found the music of J. S. Bach to be irrelevant, since it was meaningful only in a white man's culture. For good measure, he described Bach as an old goat, a has-been, and obviously not someone whose work could even remotely compare with the Supremes, a commercially prepackaged group of black girls who sing. The young man indicated no familiarity whatsoever with such eminent black composers as William Grant Still or Ulysses Kay, the noted conductor, Dean Dixon, the many renowned artists, including Leontyne Price, Marian Anderson, or others in the jazz field, too numerous to mention, who are also black. Ironically, he was as ignorant of outstanding accomplishments and contributions made to black culture by members of his own race. In one breath, this young man arrogantly asserted that persons of one race should be familiar only with activities or accomplishments by members of the same race; subjects which did not appeal to him personally were therefore "irrelevant" to the education of all men and women; and anything "new" was by definition more significant in today's society than anything old. In one brief moment, he indulged successively in racism, provincialism, and egotism. He demonstrated a profound ignorance of the accomplishments of distinguished musicians of his own race, and disrespect for the achievements of others.

The most dangerous aspect of this young man's attitude was his basic assumption that his miniscule experience and narrow degree of literacy qualified him, nonetheless, to dictate the content of his own education, or its standards.

We must draw distinctions between "criticism" of this type, and constructive criticism of another variety. If a student were to propose, for example, that adminstrators develop a program designed to provide practical experience for students in their chosen fields, such a program might contain detailed proposals intended to offer students an improved opportunity to acquire some degree of expertise in their selected areas of endeavor. The academic world is ripe for reform. But the equation of each utterance by any spoiled brat who chooses to open his mouth with intelligent, constructive suggestions by students is to invite disaster. Teachers must retain the authority to set standards and develop goals. A school in which "merit" is to be declared meaningless is a school for morons.

Similarly, teachers are individuals. They have different tastes, theories, and attitudes. A school is a microcosm of a more complex society. Student protest was advertised as an outcry against the "lawless" authority exercised by the educators, because the corporate state (i.e., society) rewards those who complete school successfully. (No one bothered to ask which students were protesting, or whether other students agreed.) Flexible curricula are desirable and essential if our educational institutions are to survive the ideological onslaught of anarchists who seek to subvert the schools to serve their own ends. But some negativists assail *all* authority because some has been abused.

Ronald Reagan has criticized the universities which function as impersonal "knowledge factories," which ignore students' individualism in pursuit of "efficiency" and a rubber-stamp variety of "education." The governor has commented, "Young men and women go to college to find themselves as individuals. They see the names of distinguished scholars in the catalogue and sign up for courses in the belief that they will learn and grow and be stimulated by contact with these men. All too often they are herded into gigantic classes taught by teaching assistants hardly older than themselves. The feeling comes that they're nameless, faceless numbers on an assembly line—green cap at one end, cap and gown and automated diploma at the other. Students want someone to know they're there."

But it is one thing to recognize the mechanized, bureaucratic injustices that exist in the academy. It is quite another to assail the idea of "merit" as a form of precipitating inequality. The most insipid criticism conceivable suggests that schools are engaged in a vast program of indoctrination designed to prepare persons for predetermined roles in an artificial society. Such characterization implies a machine of overpowering efficiency. In truth, the schools are often inefficient. Their greatest difficulty is not their diabolical cunning, but their slow, complex ways of achieving constructive change, coupled with an overpowering inefficiency and lack of direction. Administrators often demonstrate an incapacity to distinguish between growth and progress, or between expansion and improvement. We may well desire a re-examination of our definition of merit; we cannot afford the glorification of academic deterioration in the name of student–teacher equality.

Amid the confusion that pervades our society, recent trends in sociological analysis have encouraged an emphasis on expression of the "real self." Invariably, the "real self" is characterized as "honest," "unaffected," and "natural." In contrast to the qualities which the counterculture defines as manifestations of "uptightness," fear, rigidity, and an outer veneer of reserve concealing an inner self riddled with frustrations, the new "self" is portrayed as ideal.

Men and women who have discovered their "true identities" are described as relaxed, sensitive, and eager to engage in personal relationships. Artificiality and tolerance for pressures have allegedly disappeared. The social restrictions imposed by concerns for competence have vanished too. Instead, we have man in his "natural" state, free of neuroses and tensions, ready to love his fellow human beings and engage in the most meritorious forms of self-expression. Certainly, this is a highly desirable picture. But these are generalities. How are these wonderful qualities to be recognized in more specific contexts? To a sociological theoretician, being specific is to be avoided at all costs.

As an example of "uptightness," Charles Reich invites us to consider the housewives, "looking out from their windows, as if spying an unexpected patch of dirt in an otherwise spick and span house." Efforts by the police or by persons who may be characterized as "solid citizens" to identify strangers in the neighborhood who seem "different" are ridiculed as examples of "managerial paranoia."

To discern the illogic in such attitudes, we must remember that nature contains many elements which are undesirable. Some animals may be friendly to man, but thoroughly hostile to other animals. The mere "existence" of any element in nature does not justify its inclusion in a list of "desirables" for society. A skunk, for instance, is "real." It exists. It belongs to nature. We assume, too, that the skunk is "honest." Even the most rabid apologists for the youth cult would find it difficult to welcome the aroma of a skunk as a "desirable" for society. But when hundreds of young people abstain from bathing or grooming, their acquisition of their own odoriferous aroma suddenly becomes a holy crusade, a means of "liberation." In reality, these persons are being "freed" from cleanliness, and "liberated" enough to achieve a familiarity with filth. Body odor becomes "escape from artifice." Through this neat, tidy semantic sleight of hand, apologists for the new youth culture are able to make persons who bathe appear to be stodgy, frustrated, and thoroughly enslaved by the "system" or the Establishment.

Similarly, social graces become topics of amusement. The distinctions between refinement and vulgarity are obliterated. Persons who have discovered the "new self" are eager to hasten their demise. Instead, a new, imprecise, inarticulate means of expression is proposed. Deviations are not permitted. Persons who do not immediately conform to the new conversational fads are subjected to ridicule.

Young people (and their middle-aged imitators) who speak in such terminology speak of "being where its at," "grooving," "rapping," "splitting," "living at one's pad," becoming "what's happening," avoiding persons who are "uptight." The more obvious teenage examples are readily punctuated with interjections of "like this" or "like that"; sentences are interrupted constantly with "man" or "you know." Reduction of the English language to its lowest common denominator is not a discovery of teenagers. Tarzan managed to make himself understood when he said, "Me–Tarzan, You–Jane." One father managed to respond to his son's assertion, "I have to find the real me," with the suggestion, "Why don't you try looking under your hair?" A facetious answer to be sure, and one that will be denounced by the youth cult as hostile and "uptight." Such an assertion merely indicates the grim, humorless attitude that pervades the cult's adherents.

Not only is the new "vocabulary" widespread, its advocates regard its application, along with an appreciation of rock music, drugs, and long hair, as an inviolate component of a new set of mores and folkways. Woe to the young man or woman who is articulate, verbally or grammatically. Faculty psychologists will be quick to recognize that the ability to express one's self beyond the most primitive linguistic level is a manifestation of "uptightness," maladjustment, and a failure to identify with one's peer group. In other words; like, man, baby—good grammar—we'd better split and go to our pad and rap in our own way. Doing our thing is where it's at and if we want to be what's happening, it ain't grooving to use good English.

Having disposed of personal cleanliness and the English language as minor casualties, the youth cult was ready to consume bigger and better rivals. Next on the agenda was a "redefinition" or "reconstitution" of some basic moral attitudes that seem to be constantly impeding the inevitability of youthful "progress." Despite the self-righteous concern for "human relationships" which are part of the new youth culture, one of the essential elements of the "new self" is the "redefinition" of "love." Motion pictures and television, eager to capitalize on the sensationalism resulting from such considerations, assisted in burying the old institution of romance just as fast as they could find a dirty shovel.

It is easy to sneer at "romance." Attitudes regarding what is or is not romantic during a specific era may change. But the youth cult prides itself on its ability to "love." But the latter, as defined by the broadcast media and film industry, is principally a hurried effort to demonstrate how boy meets girl, and the two of them rush off to the bedroom to "do their thing." The slogan, "Make love, not war" suddenly becomes "Make sex, not war." Implicit in this original slogan was the concept that "love" (i.e., relationships based on affection, mutual respect, and commitment) was preferable to war (killing of other human beings). But when the slogan is used by apologists for the youth cult, the meaning of "Make love, not war" is clear: indulge your whims. Publicity notices for a commercially exploited play that contains considerable emphasis on nudity, declared that the production concerned "dirty" things like napalm and "clean" things like nudity and lovemaking. The producer and writers expect the audience to read a deeply profound message into this material. But the suggestion of fast, non-committal, superficial biological relationships, is anything but a suggestion of "love." Promiscuity thus becomes alternative to napalm. Why should intelligent men accept the proposition that one necessarily justifies, or is even related to, the other? The show was named appropriately, *The Dirtiest Show in Town.*

In films, free and explicit sex have become symbolic of "honesty." "Love" is reduced to those occurrences which may appear in a biology textbook. Like the dirty young man who regards his slovenly appearance as a means of "liberation," the free love advocates succeed only in clouding the issue. In their world, promiscuity becomes a virtue. Constancy becomes a vice. Apologists for the youth culture engage in clever "redefinitions," and "love," like the English language is reduced to its lowest common denominator.

We may also observe that those who trumpet the "sexual revolution" may be self-seeking in their motives. Charles Reich is eager to remind us that among the "freedoms" denied us by the corporate state are "sex exchanged between two couples, communal sex, homosexuality, and polymorphous sexual expression."

Adultery, of course, is the most basic freedom "denied us." Curiously enough, theoreticians who advocate the "new morality" can remember the "thou shalt not" aspects of killing, but not of adultery. It appears that knowledge of the Bible, like knowledge of everything else in the youth cult, is generally confined to a distinct selectivity.

The motion-picture industry and theater have become institutions for expressions of such viewpoints. Significantly, William Goldman observed in his startling book, *The Season*, that possibly one third of Broadway's plays and musicals were produced, written, or directed by a large number of homosexuals. We should not be surprised that these men applaud the assertion in *The Greening of America*, that long-haired youths do not doubt their masculinity. These men don't doubt theirs either; they haven't for a long time. But are we naïve enough to believe that the enormous community of homosexuals, many of them articulate, quite talented, and extremely influential, who have kept their private lives a secret from the public, are objective on the subject?

The key to a "redefinition" of "love" (or anything else) is to persuade society that a condition previously regarded as undesirable is actually quite ordinary. (The assumption that ordinariness and desirability are synonymous is one of the classic rationalizations of the youth cult.) Once we are persuaded that the "new morality" has a claim to normalcy, non-adherents to the new attitudes are made to feel that they are abnormal, different, and somehow wrong. The very techniques that induce conformity, abhorred by the youth cult on a superficial level, are thus used to enforce compliance. In reality, the youth cult does not find conformity distasteful, but rather conformity to ideas which are not deemed popular by self-styled arbiters of youthful taste.

By this curious indulgence in *non sequitur*, a runaway hippie girl who is willing to "love" a different boy every week suddenly becomes a "living protest against war." Prostitution has always thrived during wartime. While the girl may choose to delude herself that she is "better" than the prostitute (a pernicious retrogression to status seeking which Reich would undoubtedly deplore), her behavior, for admittedly different reasons, may be essentially the same.

Curiously, four-letter words which relate to biological functions become further manifestations of "honesty." The youth cult loves to sneer and smirk over the use of euphemisms by those whose

"Victorian morality" renders them impervious to the appeals of underground newspapers. They do not recognize the inconsistency of their assertion, on one hand, that "love" is man's highest function, and their dependence, on the other hand, on a code of social behavior that describes man's "natural" functions in the basest ways imaginable. Too often, our literature and motion pictures reflect an assumption that the most bizarre and abnormal practices of man are quite normal. We are advised that perversion is not really objectionable, so long as it constantly reflects good taste. Persons making such assertions do not recognize that perversions and immorality represent the antithesis of good taste; they are mutually exclusive.

The classic example of such misunderstanding is the assumption that any "natural function of man" is therefore appropriate at any place or time. (Again, we see the redefinition principle at work, the student who defecates in the student union reception room at Berkeley suddenly establishes a "union with nature," because he is exercising a natural function of man. Ecology is thus brought into play, and like a superpatriot wrapping himself in the flag, the unwashed rebel justifies his own perverse behavior by identifying it with some laudable causes which are totally unrelated.)

If we return for a moment to the scene of suburban tranquility misinterpreted by many, we can see how the techniques of "redefinition" can be used to examine a situation, turn it inside-out and upside-down, and ultimately persuade us that, like the audience at a magic show, we haven't seen what we've really seen at all.

The housewife is characterized as suspicious, insensitive, and afraid. Police officers are described as apprehensive and ready to assume the worst, regarding strangers. The police may be seen "investigating" those who appear "different" in the nice, clean, immaculate suburb. Finally, "solid citizens" of the suburb, men and women who are familiar with each other's ideas and personalities, reveal their prejudices and fears. In the dropout's perspective, and employing his terminology, everyone is "uptight."

If we examine the suburb more closely, however, we can see a very different picture from the one often presented to us. The housewife may work long hours in the garden, tending her flowers and planting new ones. She may have children who play on the front lawn or go around the block to join other boys and girls in the neighborhood. The same can be said for the "solid citizens" who work, pay taxes, possess a normal number of human virtues and faults, and go about their business. Into the suburb comes a young man with hair down to his shoulders. He is easily identified by an odoriferous aura; he is unkempt, unwashed, and dirty. When greeted by the townspeople, he is rude, discourteous, and quick to use obscene language. If persons try to make friendly conversation with him, he responds with a series of grunts or noises which are supposed to provide some special meaning. Why is the housewife concerned about him? First of all, he may choose to trample her flowers or defecate on her lawn. (At Berkeley, students, like dogs, learn to "do their own thing" when the impulse strikes.) He may introduce her children to obscene language or worse, to a variety of dangerous drugs. He may be addicted to drugs himself, and therefore inclined to a variety of crimes in order to support his habit. He may decide to wander around town in the nude, thus subjecting a majority of the townspeople to what *they* consider to be an indignity. (Whether this young man considers it is an indignity, or we do, for that matter, is irrelevant.) It is *their* town, because they live there, work there, and are entitled to maintain a sense of public decency if they so choose.

This does not mean that a drug pusher cannot wear a gray flannel suit. Some do. This does not suggest that a man wearing an Oriental robe and a long beard cannot be a philosopher. Many are. But in turn, critics are in no way justified in ridiculing the housewife because she wants her children safe, her lawn clean, and *her* rights protected. The police are always easy to abuse. Policemen normally meet men and women at the unhappiest times of their lives. Law violators are not happy to see policemen. Officers are human; they are not gods (or devils); they cannot make claims to either perfection or universal corruptibility. They are just men, trying to do their job, a job which is dangerous and difficult.

Police officers are abused, threatened, ridiculed, cursed, and subjected to a variety of physically intimidating attitudes. During the course of a day, a policeman may have to face rocks, bottles, physical assaults, and bullets. When the policemen are "cruising around the suburb," what are they trying to accomplish? They are obviously not trying to become wealthy. If they were, they wouldn't be on the police force. One function of the police is to protect the rights of citizens.

If the police themselves are unnecessarily violent in dealing with a suspect, they are engaged in wrongdoing themselves. Considering the pressures to which policemen are subjected today, we may well concede a human tendency toward overreaction. But to describe every incident involving a policeman's gun as "police brutality" or every episode in which an officer uses force to subdue a suspect as "authoritarian repression" is a disservice to the entire concept of law enforcement. Citizens would do well to remember that a man caught robbing a bank is not about to surrender to officers because the policeman walks up to him and says, "Like baby, let's split to the police pad and arrest you."

The most insidious implication of the unwashed conformists is their assertion that the police, by their very diligence in perusing the activities of a peculiar looking stranger in the community, are somehow engaged in wrongdoing. We are never told by anyone why this police action should be objectionable. But by innuendo and implication, we are urged to believe that such police behavior is an integral part of the massive conspiracy of the Establishment to restrict us.

In this upside-down, inside-out, never-never land, our values suddenly reverse. At America's Mad Tea Party, we are told glowingly of the toleration of young people for each other, a reverence for one's "freaky friends." In this world, it is desirable, even laudatory, to be freaky; it is reprehensible to be clean or solid. Again, redefinition procedures seek to persuade us that our natural concerns for our safety, morals, well-being, and survival are in some way "unnatural." Rising crime rates are common knowledge. Residents of the suburbs, like the cities, fear murder, robbery, rape, burglary, drug addiction, and overall moral erosion. Because we hear about so much crime, we tend to accept it as "normal." During the 1920's, the Loeb–Leopold case provoked an outcry from citizens everywhere. Public outrage was militant and widespread. Today, such a case might receive some publicity; but unless a crime achieves ghoulish proportions, like the activities of the Charles Manson family, or involves a famous public figure, notices of crime are taken matter of factly.

The youth culture has done nothing to divorce itself from crime. While superficially advertising itself as a culture based upon the innocence of children, the new life-styles of some youths have lent themselves easily to the encouragement of crime. One need only examine the statistics of crime in the Haight-Ashbury district of San Francisco (or the lawless behavior of Berkeley students and street people) to recognize this fact. The Students for a Democratic Society have often received police protection for their marches. In Chicago, they broke away from such protection and went on a rampage with bricks, chains, and clubs. At Stanford University and Columbia University, violence led to the destruction of valuable research papers and library materials belonging to distinguished scholars.

Again, we must reiterate that a community is not assuming that anyone with long hair has arrived in town to set fire to the local library or throw rocks at nearby windows. But those men and women who are aware that the youth culture, as a whole, has an execrable record regarding crime, are merely apprehensive and they should be. The egregious troublemakers and inveterate liars have created a distaste in the minds of many that carries over to affect a basic perspective of young people. Apologists should remember that the youth culture has created its own poor image; it is merely reaping the results of its ill-sown seeds.

If a group of young men and women want to move into a community and tread upon the rights of others, they may choose to disregard the egocentricity of their actions. But if the community, through its leaders, citizens, police, and elected officials, chooses to respond by inviting the young men and women to leave, the community is within its rights. In Carmel, California, a small army of hippies managed to turn a pastoral hamlet into a place where dirty vagabonds were to be seen on every street corner. The community had to place locks on all the public restrooms in town. Dogs accompanied the hippies, along with their natural involvement in the drug mystique. No community should be required to tolerate filth, drug addiction, or the indulgence of parasitic youths who expect society (i.e., the Establishment) to provide their food, shelter, and indulgence of their whims.

When citizens in Carmel responded with an efficacious program to get rid of the hippies, the hue and cry was immediately raised. Carmel residents obviously didn't understand "what the kids want."

Perhaps in a world of Mad Hatters and March Hares, sensibility and sanity may seem out of place. But in our society, we court disaster if we redefine our terms in such a way as to reverse our values. George Orwell suggested in *1984* the ultimate adoption of "newspeak," a modern terminology which would supersede real language in the totalitarian state. We don't have to wait for 1984; "open-minded reformers" are urging us, "Move right on," always, of course, in the name of progress.

The new "honesty" is, in fact, a sham. It is a foolish myth designed to persuade sane men that they are mad. In a recent Broadway play, *Butterflies are Free*, an East Village director, one of the characters in the plot, is enthusiastically promoting the "new honesty." He rattles off a long list of sordid and distasteful activities which occur in society. When he finishes, he declares to the central figure, a middle-aged lady from the suburbs, "You can't object to these. They occur as part of real life!" She responds curtly, "So does diarrhea, but I don't want to see it on the stage." Nor anywhere else, we may well add!

The new "honesty" emerges as an old artifice. Suddenly, we are presented with a new, sacrosanct youth culture. If we recognize its weaknesses, we deserve better than childish abuse.

IX.

The Youth Culture:
Evolution in Reverse

At the very heart of the youth culture, we find a confident self-assertion of righteousness. In many ways, this attitude is similar to the most rigid and restrictive viewpoints inherent in conservative religions of former times. The Puritans, we are told, took a dim view of man's pursuit of pleasure, with special emphasis on sex. The youth cult, however, reverses this stand. Everyone "must" believe in the complete moral justification of each man to pursue his whims on all matters, concerning sex or anything else. Everyone "must" approve or acknowledge the validity of anyone else's behavior. To express even the remotest doubts regarding a man's morals, his character, or the way he chooses to lead his life, is indicative of "Puritanical tendencies" or worse, "a capacity to judge others." Thus, the youth cult thrives on an artificial, arbitrary, and capricious assumption: society is expected to abolish all considerations of taste or morality in the name of "equality." Apologists for the youth cult fail to realize that their efforts to create a society in which there are no restrictions merely encourage a new form of acquiescence. Suddenly, we are faced with an inverse Puritan ethic, which requires, immediately, that we countenance all forms of sexual behavior. Dissenters are instantly labeled "Establishment," "old-fashioned," "Puritanical," or "irrelevant." A variety of derisive terms are available.

In this upside-down, inside-out world, "restrictions" are identified with "repression." The two terms are obviously not synonymous. Therefore, society is expected to yield to small groups of persons who desire no restrictions. Society, however, cannot function in a vacuum. If we abandon all private rules and guidelines for behavior, we are, in effect, enforcing the tastes and preferences of those who seek to establish an anarchistic state. Violence by high-school and college students has often been rationalized, because apologists offer the excuse that violence is perpetrated against the students themselves. Some academicians have gone so far as to suggest that violence is any assault upon the personality. Thus, the student can redefine requirements that he carry a pass to walk in the hall or attend public school until he is sixteen as a form of "violence," and respond by vandalizing the school.

Herein lies the most pernicious aspect of the youth cult: its inability to distinguish between extremes. Certainly, requirements for hall passes may be offensive to some high-school students. For openers, they offend persons intent upon cutting classes, for a variety of reasons. In most schools, education is supposed to be taking place in the classrooms, not in the halls. If a student wants to walk around in the halls, he should have a good reason. Junior-high-school boys and girls are fond of smoking, an activity that is difficult to pursue in the midst of a history lesson. High-school periods are usually brief, forty-five minutes to an hour. Teachers have enough problems today without encountering an additional one: the "right" of any "student" to wander around aimlessly in the halls, to gossip with friends about the latest favorite among local disc jockeys, to smoke, drink, or leave the school grounds at will during class time. Schools accept responsibility for minors when they open their doors to children of a community. The local principal cannot assume responsibility for the behavior of persons who may be waiting outside the school grounds seeking to "communicate" with students. In today's complex society, a student may find narcotics peddlers prowling around the fence, that would serve to illustrate the false theory of "repression." He may also find a variety of young adults who are taking time away from their usual activity, tearing up the local college campus, to pay him a visit. These persons are eager to introduce him to the joys of the unwashed revolution, if he has by some chance failed to discover them for himself. Perhaps a high-school boy's intentions outside of the classroom are not sinister at all: he may want to go across the street for a hamburger, or to visit his girl friend in another building. Rules regarding hall passes were established to prevent activities which most schools regard as undesirable and detrimental to the process of education.

Many "progressive" citizens are inclined to assume the innate beneficence of high-school students, characterized, naturally, as "the kids." We have no reason to assume that Johnny or Mary are paragons of moral virtue because they are teenagers. When critics talk about the "violence" of the high school, they fail to mention the violent and intimidating atmosphere encountered by teachers. Many instructors in urban areas have discovered to their horror that *The Blackboard Jungle* is more than the title of a successful motion picture or novel.

Society has always functioned on the assumption that men who are civilized condemn violence. Not all men are civilized, even at this late date. Our daily newspapers are quick to remind us that violence functions regularly, to the detriment of society in general. Suddenly, however, "violence" has been redefined. Hall passes and other forms of regulation are now "violent," just as violent as the forms of physical or emotional abuse we read about in the papers. (The student who protests against hall passes is expressing his outrage against war, racism, totalitarianism, and repression.) The sixteen-year-old boy who wants to smoke or drink in the restroom is presented to us a political martyr. If two teenage girls want to argue over the assertion that Mick Jagger's hair is longer than Frank Zappa's, their English teacher's insistence that they concentrate on a definition of adverbs is a manifestation of "repression" (i.e., a form of violence).

Other regulations or precedents which displease high-school boys and girls are denounced as assaults upon the self. Ultimately, this nonsense leads to the sanctity of disorder. Social observers beg the question when they make excuses about students being provoked to violence. If high-school students interpret their spelling assignments as "violence," but the students want to respond by burning all the spelling books in the school, these sympathetic adults want to invite someone else to accept the blame.

There is no denying that high schools are overcrowded and often understaffed. We cannot seriously challenge the assertion that methods of education can always be improved. We may well object to grading procedures, not because they imply "judgment," but because they provide the teacher and the pupil with an artificial goal, a symbol which often becomes more important than the process of education itself. But if we try to abolish judgment we shall fail. If each student's behavior is declared, legally, to be "equal" to every other student's behavior, with no rules, grades, standards, or qualifications, we are committing the worst judgment of all. We are engaged in the process of leveling, an artificial means of equalizing which negates, among other things, the capacity of a school to function.

In discussing the student–teacher relationship, too many students and teachers alike have assumed, by definition, that students possess the virtues of Pollyanna, while principals, teachers, or other authority figures are portrayed as having the same sensitivity we would expect in a representative of the Spanish Inquisition. Students can be troublemakers; if they are trying to initiate a revolution and replace the senior prom with a workshop on guerrilla warfare, they are inviting an authoritative (and hopefully, effective) response.

The equation of rules, grades, and an unequal student-teacher relationship with violence does a disservice to education. A non-violent society, one in which no forms of violence would be necessary, might be an idyllic utopia. But to equate sincere opposition to real violence with whimsical resistance to all forms of legitimate authority is a corruption of the word.

Ultimately, the youth cult claims to restore those aspects of the human experience which have been lost through adherence to roles, fostering of a meritocracy, and acceptance of the Protestant work ethic. Adoption of the new life-styles is supposed to represent the panacea, the solution, the cure-all which can help us to regain the lost self.

The primary purpose of these lost elements is to confuse the issue. It is easier to persuade sane men to speak out in favor of ecology, than to turn the discussion of the People's Park into a consideration of the street people and their plans to promote a municipal brand of Marxism. It is easier to talk about artistic creativity than to dwell upon the inarticulate new writers whose philosophical profundity cannot go beyond "do your own thing." It is easier to talk about freedom than to justify the bad taste which has been worn as a badge of distinction by the unwashed, foul-mouthed rabble-rousers and their neater, but terribly confused academic admirers.

By linking the counterculture with high ideals, through skillful redefinitions, psychologists and social observers can persuade us that the changes taking place in our country are perfectly normal, very much in fashion, and not worth a moment of concern. They provide the youth cult with some respectability it has been unable to acquire as a result of its own intrinsic merit. Consider some of the ways in which society is being changed today. A host of journalists and sociological speculators are applauding these changes with glee. But when the evidence is considered, we quickly see the error of their ways. Society should have regarded the youth cult for what it was: a Mad Tea Party, a costume ball, a bizarre sideshow, a cultural aberration. Instead, middle class and upper class values have been readjusted to integrate the influences of the youth cult in our social mainstream.

The cultural revolution: Participation in artistic endeavor is a noteworthy activity of which men may be proud. The explosion of creative activities on the part of young people, especially in musical and cinematic projects, is often presented as a means of proving that "the kids are all right after all." Concurrently, the adults who do not subscribe to the youth cult, those who are offended by the underground poetry in the high-school papers, the unkempt rock groups, the pseudo-pornographic films, are subjected to ridicule. They are obviously square; they are inartistic; they only understand the process of making money. But the youth cult has actively downgraded the artistic achievements of most of Western civilization. The rock-group leader who knows four chords or the creator of nonsense poetry or the avantgarde painter who takes aim at his canvas and lets the paint fall where it will are prime examples. These persons all demand the respect (and even the patronage) of society because of their inflated impressions of their own talents. But the critics and journalists who applaud these cultural advances dismiss most of the great works of art in Western civilization. Their rationale is justified by their assumption that the only relevant works of art today are those which reinforce the social or political complaints of the counterculture.

A typical example of the new culture is a poem by R. Crumb, creator of numerous underground comic books, who suggests an ideal world: a society in which every one from Peter Pan to the Pope would be "stoned," on trips induced by psychedelic drugs. Presumably the composers or writers who do not adhere to the basic doctrines of the counterculture, whose every work is not steeped in anti-Establishment propaganda, are to be dismissed. This attitude is not dissimilar to the state control over the arts that exists in the Soviet Union, where distinguished creators have been taken to task because their works do not reflect the current taste of the bureaucracy in books or music.

Advocates of the youth cult are concerned with the ability to listen to others. This is utter nonsense. Apologists for the self-styled "now" generation are constantly talking about the lack of communication. They insist that the new etiquette, the informal dress and manners, the new standards of taste, and attention to what the kids want, will establish greater communication between the generations.

They do not practice what they preach. They have demonstrated no desire whatsoever to "listen" to the views of young people who do not wear bell bottoms, beards, or long hair. Did the students of Berkeley or Columbia express an interest in listening when they turned to wanton destruction of private property, when mobs attempted to shout down faculty members who did not subscribe to their political views? No evidence has been presented to indicate that marriage, a career, or traditional moral values are mutually exclusive with meaningful, personal relationships.

If a man fosters artificial relationships, and he happens to earn a monthly salary in a specific job, nothing restrains him from re-evaluating his goals or his ideas. The youth cult thrives on the assumption that substitution of casual relationships for a marriage contract makes the relationships more "meaningful." Pursuing aimless searching instead of a career makes the former "thoughtful."

Perhaps a man has discovered what he likes to do best in the world, and wishes to pursue that career to support his family. If a man is devoted to his wife, his family, and to pursuing goals that are non-materialistic, he can achieve all of these relationships within the system. Those persons who want to abolish our institutions imply that they are no longer useful and should be discarded. This is a classic case of *non sequitur*.

Expression of the individual self through dress. Parents and teachers who favor the imposition of dress codes are constantly reminded that "today's kids are informal," that "rules of dress don't matter to them." Yet some social critics have attempted to insist that the bizarre, slovenly dress standards adopted by many young people encourage fun, work, and dignity. Dignity has never mattered to the youth cult. Nude bathing, casual free love, and perpetual existence in the unwashed state hardly encouraged dignity. Non-adherents to the youth cult have lost the capacity to dress constantly in the most primitive state available to man.

It has become fashionable to ridicule middle-aged men and women who are offended by the filth and squalor that seems to pervade the existences of the Harvard student body as much as the hippies who disappeared as fast as they left the mark on the American way of life. Different forms of dress on different occasions are denounced as a manifestation of artifice.

In other words, a man who chooses to wear the same clothing all the time is "free." Bathing suits in church become appropriate. Some advocates of the counterculture have even suggested that there is a sociological sanctity about the right to always appear bare-footed in public. We may safely conclude that Western civilization will survive, even if a majority of the populace continues to wear shoes.

The spirit of universal brotherhood. We are told that man has lost the ability to be affectionate, to care about his fellow man, to believe in brotherhood. Even if we accept these assertions as true, does our answer lie with the counterculture? Yet many American families who remain within our social mainstream are borrowing from the counterculture and emulating its exponents. The "progressive" social analysts imply that the best way to regain our values is to either emulate the youth cult, or join it. During the 1960's, news reports often seemed to indicate that dropping out was the fashion. Now the trend has changed; in the 1970's, families seem to be adopting some of the tenets of the counterculture, even as the latter fades into historical oblivion.

Drugs, for instance, dominated the hippie society of the 1960's. Today, the drug problem is significant as a major menace to our school systems. Permanent commitments to a single individual, through marriage, assumption of responsibilities relating to the family or one's career, and respect for the rights of others are all avoided by proponents of the new morality. In what ways do adherents of the new youth culture express the aforementioned qualities? Certainly not by their disregard for other people's property, tastes, and values. Rock festivals policed by motorcycle gangs do not imply brotherhood. Violent demonstrations encouraged by doctrinaire Marxists do not imply tolerance.

The drug culture. We are urged to lament the fact that the oppressive Establishment has lost the opportunity to poison itself en masse through a plethora of drugs. The result has been fewer drug addicts, fewer suicides, and fewer persons ultimately facing the agony of withdrawal.

The new morality. Despite a surplus of glib literature, immersed primarily in chic and fashionable psychological jargon, the new morality is built on an amoral view; it is inherently opposed to social morality of any type. When society expresses its own morality, through opposition to free love, nude bathing, rock festivals, dirt and filth spread by unwashed nomads, or regular dependence upon drugs by college students and a middle-aged élite, or other manifestations of the youth culture, society is subjected to vehement ridicule. The "new morality" has a neat rationale: whatever you want to do is moral, and if anyone questions you, blame it on the Establishment.

Proponents of the "new morality" cannot have it both ways. If they respect individual morality, they should cease and desist from mockery when groups of citizens express their concept of morality collectively. Such persiflage serves only to underscore the basic contempt of these social analysts for any "morality" which does not conform to popularly held notions of cult adherents and their middle-aged apologists. The morality of the youth cult is adjustable.

Many young persons choose to sneer at the Victorian morality of their elders while indulging in amoral behavior themselves. Destruction of private property, an immoral act, may be easily justified through semantic manipulations. Violence, also immoral, is similarly excused if such violence is perpetrated by adherents to the youth cult, as "defensive violence." The same rights of defense are not accorded to police or persons who are typecast as representative of the Establishment. Racism, another immoral element, is tolerated, if a manifestation of inverse racism. Persons identified with the Establishment may be ideal targets of inverse discrimination.

Respect for the law, respect for one's elders (not necessarily acquiescence, but common courtesy), respect for the property and personal rights of others, are dismissed as irrelevant. Naturally, this is not the case if the rights in question are those of the New Left, the Now Generation, or any members of the élite prepared to remake society. Angela Davis, for instance, long a heroine to youth-cult writers, can embrace communism. Yet she will avail herself of every legal privilege to secure her own freedoms under the Constitution which is diametrically opposed to her own view.

Morality is a two-way street. Too many young persons fall back on a holier-than-thou attitude when dealing with adults. The assertion "Never trust anyone over thirty" is itself discrimination, although the distinction is chronological rather than racial. We have no evidence that young persons or their middle-aged imitators are endowed with moral purity. The implication that persons who work for a living or dress conservatively are tools of the Establishment's corrupt morality is ridiculous. The age bias has been carried to its worst extreme on the high-school campuses, where student violence resulting in shootings and vandalism have become the order of the day. Laws against these activities relate to the over-thirty culture and the old morality; the "new morality" has already taken its toll.

Discussions about the "new morality" invariably turn to sex. It is a controversial subject, and it sells books or films or a variety of other products. We are told that the old morality is restrictive; instead, we can now enjoy the new freedom, which allows and encourages us to participate in a variety of sexual experiences with many different people. Fidelity is dismissed, replaced by a new casual approach which suits the whim. Critics of sex-education programs are often ridiculed and portrayed as prudish ladies in tennis shoes; but parents have cause for concern when they realize that instruction in sex-education classes may imply that morality (which is not discussed) has nothing to do with the subject. To omit discussion of prevailing moral views is to imply that these views are unimportant.

Personal fulfillment through achievement of one's own special excellence and worth. Efforts to encourage self-respect are praiseworthy. Too often, the youth cult substitutes self-satisfaction for self-respect. The result is predictable: the individual becomes smug and self-satisfied, encouraged by a society which declares (in the name of equality) that he cannot have faults or weaknesses which would render him unequal.

The concept of one's own special worth is used as an excuse to debunk excellence to encourage mediocrity. If a man wants to discover his own standard for "success," he is perfectly free to do so. If this man wants to pursue the career of a philosopher rather than that of an advertising executive, he may discover a personal definition of success. But that definition should not include an expectation that the world owes him a living, or that his creative efforts deserve to be encouraged by society simply because he thinks they are artistic and desirable.

Too often the youth cult has set itself up as an alternative to the work ethic, with the implication that those who work should be made to pay for the creative efforts of those who choose to devote their time to drugs, encounter groups, and the speeches of Jane Fonda.

Personal achievement is not highly regarded by those social observers who use the general welfare as an excuse to promote a welfare state.

The renaissance of emotion. The new youth cult is designed to perpetuate itself through a constant indulgence in man's finest emotions: bravery, courage, reverence, and romance. Yet the coarse, neurotic youth culture was built on disrespect for tradition, conformity, irreverence, and an assumption of infallibility. It is hardly capable of restoring these qualities.

The youth culture is the antithesis of romance. The art, music, and literature of the unwashed masses emphasizes realism. The underground press eschews refinement, taste, and respect. A culture which regards a four-letter obscenity as the best expression of one's feelings is hardly romantic, by anyone's definition.

In recent months, trends have changed. As an option for those who do not totally embrace the New Left or the counterculture, psychologists have suggested an alternative. Marriage, we are told, is an outdated institution; but it can be revitalized, they continue, through the use of a marriage contract, in which both parties agree to a complex legal arrangement; part of the arrangement is a statement of the rights and privileges of both persons, with special emphasis on the right of the wife to study karate or make speeches urging the abolition of men, or other appropriate activities for the liberated woman. If a married couple must engage in more complicated negotiations than the Paris Peace Talks in order to get married, the new marriage is a dubious institution. The marriage contract concept is an example of pseudo-intellectual efforts to accept the assertion of the counterculture during the 1960's (i.e., marriage is extinct) and to apply it to the 1970's. The difficulty arises from the fact that the youth cult of the 1960's was an aberration; marriage and the family must be revitalized, not destroyed or rendered inadequate.

Assumption of responsibilities is often unpleasant; the adult world is riddled with inconsistences, hypocrisies, and faults of all shapes and sizes. The search for the true self is complex; it cannot be ended by the assertion that a panacea for the human condition can best be realized through the adoption of dress, music, jargon, and complete capitulation to teenage whims. Grace and Fred M. Hechinger declared, in their book, *Teen-Age Tyranny*, "What worries us is not the greater freedom of today's youth, but rather the abdication of the rights and privileges of adults for the convenience of the immature. As a result, American society is growing down rather than growing up."

Before our search for the real self can be successful, we must assure ourselves that growth and attitudes progress in the right direction, not the wrong way.

X.

The Decaying of America:
The Youth Cult Revolution

When the term "revolution" is introduced into a conversation, most Americans picture a violent upheaval. We imagine a scene out of Dickens, with French nobles being marched off to the guillotine, and an eager Mme. DeFarge knitting furiously in the front row. When Americans think in terms of "revolutionaries," they often imagine sinister terrorist plots and clandestine meetings. Certainly revolutionaries of this sort do exist in contemporary society. But some theoreticians suggest that the youth cult represents a new form of social change, in which individuals change their own lives, and concurrently change society. In theory, at least, the idea seems to make sense. If enough individuals were to decide to become vegetarians, for example, the meat industry would have a problem. Meat packers do not concern themselves with this possible crisis, because they think that universal adoption of vegetarian ideas is highly unlikely.

At least for public consumption, the youth cult has advertised itself as non-violent, changing the political structure as its final act rather than as its initial *coup d'etat*. Instead, we are constantly reminded that the culture of "our young people" is a renaissance of the American spirit, a collective movement of individual acts which, when combined, will ultimately express the best ideals of the American dream. Such an assertion, while very desirable and optimistic, is easily proven to be superficial. The suggestion of a new renaissance of the American spirit implies that we have somehow gotten away from our heritage, our roots, our basic

185

principles. If we believe what we are told, the life-styles of certain young people—their taste in clothing, style, and manner, their use of drugs and dependence upon sex, their music, and ideological leanings toward collectivist philosophy—will lead us back to the things we have lost. But by definition, the youth culture is *against* perpetuation of a strong family unit, *against* traditional moral values, *against* most of the principles and ideals that have formed our social foundation. If the youth cult emerges triumphant, it will herald not the dynamic renewal of the American dream, but the beginning of its ultimate decline.

To realize why this is the case, we must remind ourselves that many of the worst crimes in the history of civilization have been perpetrated in the name of idealistic goals: "freedom," "peace," "liberty," "religion"; religious wars or rivalries stimulated by religious hatred or bigotry have been among the bloodiest and most violent of man's conflicts. Ostensibly, these religious wars and rivalries have been led by men seeking to spread "God's word." The fact that their violence is perpetrated in the name of idealism or benevolence makes it no less violent.

The self-styled cultural revolution known as the "counter-culture" has been based on certain assumptions. A brief examination of these assumptions reveals that they are shallow slogans with no real factual depth. Before examining the real meaning of the ways in which advocates of the new youth culture want to change our society, it is advisable to consider some of these myths.

One myth is that the United States is a corporate state in which persons who try to speak the truth about its nature are intimidated. This is utter nonsense. Despite all propaganda efforts to the contrary, persons in the United States are more free to express themselves than in any other country in the world. What is meant by intimidation or harassment?

Eldridge Cleaver and LeRoi Jones are cases in point. Certain legal moves were required to prevent Cleaver from assuming a faculty position at Berkeley, a post for which he was legally unqualified. The first amendment does not include the "right" of any man to necessarily teach credit courses at a tax supported university. A man who has spent his life as a plumber is not being denied his "right of free speech" because he is not invited to lecture at a university medical school or to teach business classes at Harvard.

Why are apologists for the youth cult always upset about the "infringement" upon the right to be obscene? Do they really believe that filthy speech is the only meaningful cause that exists in our society? The American Civil Liberties Union may indulge in legal difficulties over definitions. A firm, precise definition of legal obscenity may be difficult to obtain. Attorneys are well aware of the controversies that surrounded the McNaughton rule for years, relating to the legal definition of insanity. The underground press evidently is hard-pressed for words, because in expressing itself on all subjects, journalists of the counterculture seem always to require the same small groups of nouns, verbs, and adjectives. If writers and filmmakers are successful in blurring the legal restrictions on obscenity, they prove only that in the United States they have the legal right to be coarse or crude in public. In setting up a list of priorities for reform in this country, is the right of a man to be obscene (or publicly offensive) of such great priority? Self-styled civil libertarians are adept at quoting Jefferson while trying to justify the writings of playwright Michael McClure. They quote the Constitution, the Bible, and an assortment of fine observations about free speech; but their crusade is often in behalf of pornographic films.

The Establishment is violent and depends on violent repression to enforce its will. "Police brutality" has become an odd cliché these last two decades. In the past few years, professors have become distraught over the presence of police officers on campus. Does a single, solitary reason exist which justifies lawlessness, simply because such illegal acts occur on college property? "Academic freedom" is a term which historically has implied the right of teachers to practice their art without intimidation or restriction, so long as they remain within the law and within the conditions of their employment by the university. Academic freedom has never incorporated a license to disobey the law. Why should college students be exempt from the laws that govern society simply because they walk through a college gate?

Apologists for perpetrators of student violence seem to think that a highly desirable state of affairs exists if a group of students decide to declare the laws "irrelevant" by disobeying them collectively. The idea is not a new one, and even conservative students have read Thoreau and studied the speeches of the Reverend Martin Luther King, Jr. But if students decide to take the law into their own hands or destroy private (or public) property, non-violent protest goes out the window.

The curious rationale offered as an excuse implies that the laws become meaningless because they are disobeyed. Imagine that a union decided to declare the laws regarding strikes "irrelevant," and burned down the office buildings of companies that did not accede to their demands. Imagine a large industrial plant that considered federal regulations "irrelevant" and willfully distributed defective merchandise or dumped massive quantities of industrial waste into a public water supply. Most of all, consider the individual citizen who decides that laws against private property are "irrelevant," and appropriately helps himself to a television, automobile, and money belonging to someone else.

A society in which individuals can disobey the laws simply by declaring them "irrelevant" is a society which is courting chaos. This dangerous tendency toward lawlessness is unrelated to theories of non-violent protest, ostensibly derived from Thoreau, in which individuals were prepared to take their punishment for violating a law in order to protest its existence. At State University at Stony Brook, Long Island, police enforced the narcotic laws to protect citizens who do not wish to become part of the drug culture.

The students at Stony Brook stoned police cars, set fires, pelted the fire trucks that came to put out the fires, and broke two hundred windows. Students were reportedly incensed over the use of police informers. Obviously those involved in the drug traffic were not going to turn themselves in to the police. Yet the police were popularly characterized as villains, "violent tools of the Establishment's repression." The students' initiation of violence is thus characterized as a manifestation of police harassment. Attention is thus focused on police informers, not the persons violating drug laws. The police could have allowed the drug laws to be violated and permitted the campus to burn down, but presumably they decided to be "repressive" on behalf of the majority of students who still wanted to attend classes.

The Establishment is hostile to the youth culture. Society is assumed to be innately suspicious of the quality of books, films, or music, which is steeped in the revolutionary doctrines of the counterculture. This is utter nonsense. To the contrary, society today makes things harder for those young people who do not subscribe to the counterculture. Middle-aged adolescents are usually quick to assume the inherent quality and "goodness" of music, art, or creative writings, if these works have been produced by members of the younger generation. The assumption equates "newness" with "progress." Because a motion picture or novel is recent, these persons automatically endow its creator with "progressive" qualities. They specifically discount (or ignore) the possibility that the work is simply not as good as an older, less "innovative" book or film.

The Establishment perpetuates itself through the maintenance of unfair, biased "hierarchies" that imply the inequality of participants.

Status emerges from human relationships because men are basically unequal. They possess different talents, abilities, and capabilities. Some men are able to assume many responsibilities; others are unable to meet even the slightest professional obligations. In any society, the emergence of leaders and followers is predictable, and in no way a basic deterrent to freedom. Such distinctions should be based on ability, not race, creed, or religion.

The new youth culture will dictate to the mass-marketing interests, because if "the kids" only want bell-bottoms, manufacturers will have to sell them or lose sales.

Again, this conclusion is based upon the premise that the market is established through popular demand for products. Most of the fads and fashions of the youth cult have been created through advertising and public-relations campaigns. Admittedly, some of these campaigns have been launched by men and women who dress differently or who use different jargon than advertising or promotional executives of ten years ago. But despite the outward differences, these persons have not been interested in "responding to the popular demand"; instead, they have taken over commercial channels of communications for the same reasons as their predecessors: the sale of their products and their personal profit. Promoters of rock groups, for example, may wear bell-bottoms or beards, but as businessmen their attitudes are indistinguishable from their older, less aggressive colleagues who now seek to imitate them.

The key, therefore, to assessing the real worth of a revolution, even a non-violent revolution, is not an evaluation of what it overthrows, but rather what it offers. Too often one form of totalitarian regime is replaced by another totalitarian regime. Our society, of course, is anything but totalitarian; with all its faults, which we may freely acknowledge, we should think *more* than twice before wholeheartedly replacing it with another social order. Social observers respond to the milder indiscretions and blatant immorality of some young people by talking about the "searching" generation; they emphasize general, passive activities, "searching," "knowing," "feeling," "experiencing." Active, creative, dynamic, specific programs and proposals are usually ignored. The youth cult has developed no concrete individual philosophies or credos, any more than it has developed broadly based doctrines for social reform.

The youth cult, with its emphasis on dropping out is based on the assumption that individual changes will alter the entire society. Such conversion might be legitimately compared to the adoption of a religious belief by a single individual. If enough individuals subscribe to the new life-styles, we are told that these life-styles will ultimately be adopted by the majority. But we can assess the success or failure of these individual life-styles collectively. With the decline of such hippie havens as Haight-Ashbury, emphasis has been less upon dropping out of society and more upon the absorption of counterculture life-styles (music, dress, and morals) in our social mainstream. Herein lies the danger. Society will not fall apart because of a few dropouts, but it may decline through adoption of a whole variety of detrimental influences. If we examine the youth culture as a whole, what do we find?

Political dogma steeped in Marxism, little respect for individual freedom, a willingness to exploit racial differences. When forced into a concrete declaration of principles, the advocates of our "young people" offer standard, shopworn, Marxist political dogma. Even high-school students are mouthing tired old collectivist slogans. These are hardly the "new" or "exciting" answers to our social and political ills. These solutions have failed in Russia and China. The apolitical revolution is steeped in collectivism, with all its well-known evils.

The youth cult offers to replace our "culture" with its own. What is the new music, art, literature, or poetry? In the artistic fields, in which the advocates of the youth cult have enjoyed free reign, what have we been offered as an alternative? A "musical art form" in which we assume profundity to be implicit in the caterwauling of anyone who plays the guitar and tries to sing? Painting which requires no special skills, or pop art which presumably tells us that our society is irrelevant. Literature or films in which a heavy emphasis upon sex and drugs is considered to be the *only* meaningful approach to any subject! An approach to the English language in which literacy is regarded as an affectation and illiteracy is glorified as an expression of the true self! In truth, the new "culture" is not the blissful product of "participants" working, as their advocates would have us believe, out of individual creative expression, rather than technical skills.

This is the "culture" of a new social order which not only glorifies dilettantism, but implies that the work of commercially exploited illiterates or amateurs is superior to the work of anyone who is skilled. In the musical profession, even the most distinguished composers have been forced out of work to make room for unskilled persons who play the guitar or sing with no special talents or abilities. The new "culture" is supposed to be noncompetitive; in reality, it is a competitor. Writers of non-sensational novels or screenplays are already encountering difficulties similar to those which hastened the professional demise of many fine composers. If their works do not conform to the youth-oriented syndrome developed by an open-minded, "non-competitive" élite, these writers can forget their careers too. In the new youth culture, the brilliant artist and the impudent ignoramus are equal; if the former does not express his "equality" by imitating the latter, he is eliminated.

The new youth cult replaces refinement and dignity with crudity, casualness, and impudence. In the new youth cult, presumably dominated by "affection" or "mutual respect," Social graces are regarded as "affectations"; so are all forms of courtesy or refinement. Youthful arrogance does not allow for the fact that all of the *progress* as well as the negative elements in our society was achieved by former generations.

The youth cult replaces cleanliness with filth. Charles Reich speaks glowingly of the day when the President of the United States "will have to don bell-bottoms and a dirty shirt" and go searching for his constituents. Advocates of the new "culture" are not in the least disturbed by the implication that activities exist in the realm of human endeavor which require reverance, dignity, personal cleanliness, or serious and respectful demeanor. According to the new "culture" man can play the same "role" everywhere, all of the time. But man is not fulfilling the same functions twenty-four hours a day.

The youth cult replaces order with disorder. Its adherents often like to assume that "order" implies repression because it provides an easy and accessible excuse to applaud disorder. Rock groups have been offered as an example of the ideal, communal way of life. The feuds, lawsuits, and petty disagreements that have permeated the professional associations of these groups are a matter of public record. Promoters of such gatherings are quick to publicize them as "celebrations of life," implying that middle America and conservative parents should be eager to apologize for misunderstanding their intentions. Yet these "celebrations" are a prime example of the youth cult's ineptitude.

In Puerto Rico, thirty thousand youngsters attended a rock festival. The result? Three hundred hippies at the airport without funds and unable to return home. The festival included three drownings, a murder, and a considerable number of lesser crimes. A Miami newsman said he was nearly knocked off his feet by "the stench of marijuana." These young people advertise their complete inability to participate in an orderly society every time they attend such a gathering. In Puerto Rico, the civil defense organization had to be called in for help.

Legitimate status distinctions are replaced by new, artificial distinctions, based not on merit or achievement, but on "implied equality." Status distinctions are supposed to represent the dependence of society upon artifice and formality. This dependence serves to perpetuate the Establishment. We are told that doctors behave as if they are "superior" to nurses, bosses behave as if they have the right to "boss" their employees, teachers have authority over their students, etc. Ostensibly to dignify the working man, we are advised to forget about the authority of one individual over another.

This neat ideological bubble is quick to burst. The only alternative to a society that preserves status distinctions is a society run by an endless number of committees, composed presumably of persons who have been stamped, sealed, and certified "equals." A major university in mainland China is run on this basis, with the top administrators responsible to a non-college graduate, a people's representative. (We can imagine the outcry if the faculty of Harvard were made responsible to a "hardhat.") In truth, we cannot obliterate differences in ability or leadership potential by pretending that the formal trappings of authority have been abandoned. A good teacher must take charge of his class, regardless of whether he tries to be friendly with students. If this non-status approach were carried to its logical extreme, surgeons would allow interns and nurses to express an equal diagnostic voice in the operating room. Pilots, who exercise obvious control over whether the plane goes up or down, east or west, will suffer a similar fate. Passengers and stewardesses would be able to operate the controls. In school, kindergarten students could vote to decide whether or not they want to read, write, or spell, and devote themselves to the less strenuous activities of life. Ultimately the folly of artistic incompetents and ignoramuses could be extended to all forms of human endeavor. In government, important decisions could be made by thousands of additional committees instead of individuals. Umpires would be eliminated from sports, with decisions made "equally" by fans, depending on who screams loudest.

The use of the uneducated to oversee the activities of professors would be an effective way of seeing that they did not veer far from state-approved "people's policies." Those who seek to abolish all forms of authority are really trying to transfer authority to themselves. The society controlled by "people's committees" is really controlled not by the people but by the bureaucrats, functioning under orders from those who successfully control the bureaucracy. Cries of "black power" or "student power" often emanate from those who seek power not for blacks or students, but for themselves as the self-appointed spokesmen for a group. Society must have leaders and followers. Inequities do exist, and these should be corrected, but not by pretending to abolish "status," so that employees or students can declare themselves "leaders" of groups which never elected them, as an excuse to exploit society for their own gain.

The youth cult reverses leadership roles between the generations. Parents are expected to devote their time to purging themselves of a collective sense of "guilt." They regard their children as guileless and virtuous, and consider the "progressive" life-style of their offspring to be sacrosanct. Parents thus become followers, seeking to emulate their children in order to relieve their sense of "guilt" regarding the ills of the world. The younger generation assumes the lead; the question is not whether the children can grow up to follow the ideals of their parents, but whether the parents can somehow obtain the "approval" of the younger generation by admitting their guilt and eliminating it by subscribing to the tenets of the youth cult.

Naturally, the parents are encouraged to regard ideas which conflict with the new culture as old-fashioned and irrelevant, by definition. If the youth cult is founded upon cultural illiteracy, abstention from personal cleanliness, drug addiction, or amoral social values, these elements are granted a new respectability because they are identified with youth. The idea of parents following the spiritual beneficence of their "innocent" children might be valid if members of the younger generation were either "innocent" or "children." But this standard does not apply to adherents of the youth cult. A pair of middle-aged parents whose greatest aim in life is to identify with youth through adoption of long hair, long sideburns, mini-skirts, bell-bottoms, teenage jargon, dependence on drugs, and a futile search for the fountain of youth are making fools of themselves. Parents should be concerned about setting good examples for their children, not assuming that "what the kids want" is necessarily right and proper just because children are chronologically closer to achieving the state of youth. Fathers and mothers should be interested in being leaders, not imitators. They have better things to do with their time than constantly wondering if they have managed to go "where it's at." The fact that a man of fifty succeeds in growing sideburns which were popularly grown to that length during the days of Chester A. Arthur or William McKinley does not mean that he is "young" or that his ideas about raising children are necessarily correct.

The youth cult proposes to replace "the system" with a "systemless society." Unfortunately, society cannot survive without systems. If all governments were abolished, private individuals would invariably try to seize power. The youth movement reputedly encourages men to "roll in the grass and lie in the sun." No one explains who is going to pay for these individuals' well-being. Unless they begin receiving welfare checks out of other men's pockets, their source of income becomes a matter of public concern. If they can support themselves, their life-style is their own business, to the degree that their behavior does not infringe upon the rights of others. But persons do not live in a vacuum. If they choose to wander around without visible means of support, they cannot be permitted to become public nuisances. Some suggest that individuals selecting their vocations should not be intimidated by whether such a choice represents an established occupation, defined and accepted by society. This is all very well and good in theory; but in practice, careers which are not "established occupations" may well infringe upon the general welfare of other citizens. A man has a perfect right to consider himself a poet if he so chooses; but if his pursuit of *la vie bohéme* means that he may expect hardworking citizens to support him, or to pay for his food and clothing by stealing, his life-style is treading upon the rights of others.

The youth cult fosters an adjustable moral standard, in reality a double standard used to exonerate its adherents or justify the very acts on their part that they condemn in others. One cannot divorce the youth movement from its political agitators or the chaotic violence of rock festivals. We cannot pretend that the new "culture" is divorced from its more unpleasant advocates. Society cannot pretend that Jerry Rubin's obscenities are "meaningful" simply because he chooses to wrap himself in a cloak of idealistic respectability. Advocates of the youth cult are quick to condemn "violence" or "immorality" among police officers, businessmen, or hardhat construction workers. They are careful never to do so when referring to campus mobs or drug peddlers.

The implication that the "revolution of the now generation" is divorced from violence and immorality is hollow indeed. In truth, the new youth movements represent a headlong flight from responsibility. "Morality" does not signify doing whatever is pleasant or fashionable at the moment. Until the youth cult repudiates its dependence on drugs, obscenity, filth, squalor, and violence, we can only regard its "revolutionary" potential as equivalent to the outcry of spoiled children. These are not children, however, but young adults, fully capable of dismantling our society and replacing it with one of their own.

The youth cult ignores the forgotten Americans. Thousands of persons of all ages want the "good life." They want peace, freedom, and opportunity to find the best mode of living for themselves and their families. Foremost among the forgotten Americans are the young people who do not adhere to the tenets of the youth movement. A college student who does not choose to follow his "leaders" on campus may be subject to social or political ostracism by students or faculty who may possess influence. The young executive who does not give the impression that he is a "bright, young man," fully communicative with "the kids" and "what they want" may be started on the road to professional failure. The parent who tries to maintain discipline, respect, or an intelligent perspective regarding the "old" values may be subjected to the full retaliation of the permissive society.

The youth cult venerates an élite group of "heroes" who become the favored few and models for emulation. Although the youth cult ostensibly deplores status seekers, it encourages the mass adulation of false idols who often possess no redeeming qualities whatsoever. Leaders of rock groups, anarchists, and even Communists become nationally known celebrities who enjoy fame, publicity, lucrative lecture fees, television and radio coverage, and popularity. Although these "heroes" often dress in old clothes or feign identification with the "common man," they function as stars, often enjoying a life-style which is as ostentatious as that of film stars of yesteryear.

When former Beatle, John Lennon, and his wife, Yoko Ono, were facing deportation from the United States, television comedian Dick Cavett hurried to the rescue. He testified before a Congressional committee that these "creative" people represented an example to which every young couple in America could aspire. Lennon, in previous interviews, freely admitted that the Beatle tours consisted mainly of free women, liquor, and drugs, reminiscent of a Roman orgy. Cavett, a Yale graduate, whose show is supposed to appeal to a "sophisticated" audience, saw no discrepancy between his evaluation of Lennon and the ex-Beatle's admitted reputation.

Admittedly, society has often indulged in hero worship directed at unworthy persons. But never before have so many popular idols deliberately flaunted their veritable lack of a moral code in the public's face. We would hardly expect someone with an inquiring mind to present Richard Wagner, for instance, as an example of what every young man should be. Wagner was a great musical genius and a brilliant composer, but his personal behavior left much to be desired. The current "creative" idols are fortunate to possess even minimal musical or literary ability, let alone superior skill. Yet these people are presented constantly to impressionable teenagers as examples of successful, ideal human beings; in teenage parlance, they "have it made." Elementary logic should make it obvious to Cavett and his cohorts that a society that regards the Beatles as its most honored "achievers" is a society turned upside-down.

Similarly, vast amounts of attention and financial rewards are directed toward radicals like Jerry Rubin or Angela Davis. Though possessing no real programs or proposals, these people are elevated to the exalted status of political pundits; they may be regarded as ideological curiosities at best. In truth, they seek only to incite the public to destroy the very system which permits them to speak. In the youth cult, political irresponsibility or lack of artistic ability are prime requisites for achievement of stardom and recognition as an opulent, flamboyant celebrity "forced" to enjoy his fame.

The most unfortunate aspect of this new hero worship is its effect on the younger generation. In former times, young people grew up idolizing men and women who had achieved something meaningful in government, science, the arts, or even sports. Great figures in American history (i.e., Jefferson, Lincoln, etc.) could be regarded as examples of the best that our country could produce.

Today, however, as the youth cult debunks our history and culture, and anyone or anything not part and parcel of the "keep young" movement, we see the results. If Angela Davis can become an honored celebrity by joining the Communist party, why shouldn't eleven-year-old Mary take a good look at communism? If Jerry Rubin can become a "famous author" by writing a book in which one entire page is filled with obscenities and nothing else, why should twelve-year-old Johnny bother studying literature? Although we are constantly told that each generation of children grows into a progressively more sophisticated generation of teenagers, we tend to forget that young people can be as impressionable and as conformist-oriented as a flock of sheep. Consider the frustrated teenagers down the block who resent the millions of dollars earned by their equally untalented counterparts on television. Consider the justifiably frustrated young men and women at college who cannot find a forum for their views because they are too responsible to merit the attention of those who publicize and promote only the sensational. Such emulation can only court distorted values.

Those who talk incessantly about the Establishment fail to credit the youth culture with its greatest success. Although many young people oppose the cult, American society today is engaged in its own destruction by a pernicious effort to subject every social and cultural component to the standards and capricious whims of the new youth movement. It is a revolution steeped in irresponsibility, vulgarity, and childish temperament. It is a revolution that seeks not a renaissance of ideals, but a new social order under the cloak of idealism. It is a revolution which demands conformity to all its mores and folkways. It is a revolution to which many "mature" Americans seem eager to capitulate. It is a revolution which easily identifies what it is against, but not what it advocates. It is a revolution that glorifies the primitive and debases the civilized. It is a revolution that functions in a moral vacuum. It is a revolution that seeks to destroy our society, debunk our culture, and degrade our values. It is a revolution that seeks to accomplish these things by accusing non-believers of the cardinal sin: the crime of maturity. It is a young revolution, an evil revolution, and though some of its adherents possess the best intentions, we must remember all too well where the road of good intentions can lead.

XI.

Blueprint for Progress: A Positive Answer to the Youth Cult

If we cannot find the answers to today's problems in the creation of a youth cult, we must discover solutions somewhere else. It is easy enough to recognize the weaknesses in theories advanced by radicals or to laugh at the foolishness of middle-aged adolescents who applaud them. This is the first step; the second and most important step, however, may be achieved by the substitution of a legitimate interpretation of these same events. There is no panacea, no instant solution. But positive alternatives do exist; it is our duty to discover them and our responsibility to see that they are not obscured by simplistic rationalization or childish tantrums.

The greatest danger presented by the youth cult becomes apparent when we realize that a number of its suppositions in regard to society are true. Men are often preoccupied with materialistic goals; they are often immoral and hypocritical. Our priorities have often become confused; our life-styles have not brought us instant happiness. Unfortunately, as has been demonstrated in previous pages, the youth cult itself is actually a negative, highly deleterious result of our confusion. The youth cult is founded on the assumption that any number of elements identified with social progress go together. This is false. Often mature adults are drawn to the youth cult in spite of the fact that the new "culture" stands for all the qualities they may abhor. We may discern a blueprint for progress by calling upon our common sense and mature intelligence to recognize our current social difficulties for what they are.

In every instance in which a society which depended on the "old values" has created difficulties for itself, it has actually ignored the "old values" while pretending to uphold them. Thus, we see quickly that our institutions are not at fault, but rather, our human tendencies to do those institutions a disservice. Therefore, let us seek to achieve the following:

. . . Distinguish between change and progress. Ideas are not "good" because they are "new" or "bad" because they are "old." War, poverty, immorality and disease are as "old" as time. They are as "new" as yesterday's newspaper.

. . . Recognize that time-honored principles and traditions are often time honored because they work. We must constantly recall an important corollary of this principle: a return to "old" values does not necessarily imply retrogression.

. . . Be certain that if institutions are to be abolished or replaced, they will be succeeded by other institutions of greater value to society.

Advocates of the new culture insist that the status (or survival) of our political and economic institutions is irrelevant and insignificant until individual life-styles change.

It has become intellectually fashionable to leap before you look. We court disaster if we discard institutions, without the foggiest notion of how these elements will be replaced. Our positive response is to re-examine these institutions and to improve them. If marriages have often ended in divorce or unhappiness, the youth cult adherents say, "Marriage is out. Eliminate marriage." This is clearly a flight from responsibility. If marriages have not worked over long periods of time, it is because men and women have not made them work. If families are not close, middle-aged adolescents are quick to declare that "It's because parents don't understand what the kids want."

They beg the question. Family relationships do not work well because something is wrong, and that something is far more complex than the satisfaction of youthful idealism. One positive step is the assumption of responsibility by members of the family unit. Fathers and mothers would do well to consider the confusion that results when both parents are busily pursuing full time careers. Parents should start setting examples for the children, not the other way around.

Lawrence H. Fuchs, who teaches a college seminar on the American family, has insisted that the American family will re-emerge as a triumphant institution of the 1970's. He observes, "People can only hurt so long. The pain the young are feeling makes them more realistic. As they watch the wreckage around them, they seek loving and belonging. When they find no alternatives that really work, and there are none, they will think of ways to strengthen the family." We cannot sit idly by, watching our institutions fall apart; what is true regarding the family is equally true of other institutions. Only a fool would try to deny that a variety of individuals, violent and extreme, would like to see our society destroy itself. Their goal, of course, is an opportunity for them to rebuild society according to their own whims. Civilized man has come to depend upon institutions because he cannot afford to be so fatalistic as to depend upon the innate "goodness" of all other men.

We are told that, "Schools are imperfect. Tear down the schools." Nonsense! Of course, they're imperfect. Let us improve them. (In many instances, the schools can be improved by a return to some of the tested principles that made the schools successful in the first place. If colleges and universities seem to provide training which is irrelevant, educators can provide alternatives.) We are also told that, "The government is imperfect. Abolish the government." Nonsense! If we abolish the government, who will govern? No one, suggests the anarchist. Everyone will live together in one big happy society, one marvelous rock festival of love, peace, and brotherhood. But adherents of the youth cult have demonstrated time and time again that their perfect, "systemless society" of rock festivals leads to utter chaos. The free indulgence in drugs and sex is not a discovery of this generation; ultimately, the youth cult's solution to our institutional problems is to ignore them. Instead, we are told that these problems will work themselves out after we all renounce the values of the Establishment. The rock festival is as new as the Roman orgy, and as deadly.

We are told that many of our political figures are frauds,

insufferable windbags and blithering hypocrites. Like all societies, we have our share. If we want to get rid of incompetent politicians, we possess the ways and means to do so. We are told that our democracy or our republican system is a myth, that only the rich and the powerful can exert political pressure. Perhaps we need to discover new ways to influence public opinion. The civil-rights movement of the 1950's and 1960's and the public lobbyists representing conservationists are examples of constructive political action. What better means exist to eliminate incompetent political figures? In some countries, they would be exiled or shot, with similar treatment for their supporters. Some choose to tell us that, "Idealism justifies our violence." Translated, this is equivalent to "The end justifies the means." True, Mussolini made the trains run on time, but we would be hard pressed to find excuses for his methodology.

. . . Recognize distinctions between constructive criticism and destructive action. Lenin once said that it would be irrelevant for two-thirds of the world to perish so long as the remaining third accepted total communism. A "community of scholars" in which restroom graffiti represent profound cultural expression is hardly constructive. Neither are the idealization of promiscuity, drug addiction, or strong-arm political methods. The unwashed malcontents on our campuses should curb their inclinations toward public defecation and learn to govern themselves before taking on the rest of the world.

What is the difference between constructive and destructive criticism? The former is offered in a positive spirit, with some sense of clear desire to improve or to build. The destructive critic has only vague slogans to promulgate, not specific suggestions. Indeed, the one offering destructive criticism is not interested in suggesting or proposing, but in demanding. The constructive critic says, "Let us improve our school curricula by recognizing that each student is an individual and that we need not sacrifice standards in order to make general education requirements more flexible in degree programs." The destructive critic says, "All power to the people! My group demands power to change the schools to suit us!" It is not very difficult to distinguish between the two varieties.

. . . Encourage action based upon positive goals, not a sense of collective guilt. Many well-meaning individuals render themselves incapable of exercising a positive influence even to the smallest degree. The nugatory middle-aged adolescents are so eager to please, so willing to prove their desire to purge themselves of guilt, so ready to be "open-minded," that they render themselves ideologically impotent.

We are confronted by a situation that is unparalleled in American history. Today, if certain "young intellectuals," were to suggest to certain middle-aged citizens that they could cleanse themselves of their "guilt" by jumping into the lake, the response would be predictable: the middle-aged morons would be quick to reply: "Thanks, kids. Which lake should we jump into?"

Al Capp has suggested that the ultimate protest will come when kindergarten students hear the call and protest the denial of the right of four-year-olds to see Elliott Gould in the nude at the movies, "a privilege millions of other Americans are free to enjoy." The point is well-taken.

. . . Acknowledge that alternative life-styles exist as practiced by non-conformist young people. We refer, of course, to the real non-conformists, those who refuse to join the conformist youth cult. Middle-aged apologists are often eager to dichotomize, to divide society into a neat bipartite division: old fogies and progressives; bigoted conservatives clinging to antedeluvian glories and kindly, beneficent professors who wear long hair and understand "what the kids want." This simplistic approach to sociology is convenient because it divides society into a handy group of heroes and villains who may be easily identified by speech, manner, and dress. Fortunately, such divisions do not hold up under close scrutiny.

Many young Americans do not espouse the radical, irresponsible politics or bizarre behavior which are popularly associated with the younger generation. It is unfortunate that these young people must constantly defend themselves as "squares" or "conformists." In a society that bends itself over backward to publicize its radicals, the conservative becomes the true non-conformist for he fails to run with the pack. The primitive world of the dropouts of the 1960's was portrayed as the future society, an image of progress. The true non-conformists recognize that the counter-culture had nothing to offer in the first place, so there is little reason for society to emulate it. The hippie sub-culture repre-sented chaos; now we are advised to emulate that sub-culture in mainstream society, ignoring its primitive, retarded nature. The dropouts conformed to a society which rejected all meaningful values. Those young people who held onto their values during these turbulent times are the real future leaders of America. They deserve to be recognized as such, not dismissed as members of the Establishment who are too unsophisticated to recognize the worth of psychedelic anarchy as Paradise Lost.

. . . Re-examine our sense of values. One does not have to be young to recognize dishonesty or hypocrisy in business. If we cheat on our taxes, we are being dishonest. If we cheat or lie in business dealings, we are being hypocritical. The great error of the counterculture was the assumption that its own prejudicial dogma is an automatically required alternative to these unethical forms of behavior. The drug culture has no relationship with honesty in business. Neither does the glorification of slobbism.

The dropout society was riddled with violence and misery. Many young people are beginning to realize that dropping out of society is not the answer, and that our nation can improve through constructive, positive action. But laudatory goals cannot be achieved if we welcome to the mainstream of society in the 1970's those elements of the dropout culture who could not survive the 1960's. We need more than a muddled apology for the drug mystique, the brutal anarchists of the New Left, the artificially prepackaged pop culture which debunks excellence, the obscenity, irresponsibility, and filth which permeates the youth cult.

Kenneth Kenniston, Professor of Psychology at Yale, has stated that "culture has been so far too much of a counterculture, too much defined by opposition to the evils which you correctly perceived in American society, too much an outcry against our culture's failure to fulfill its promises or to build upon its achievements. The student movement, for understandable reasons, has so far largely been a movement of opposition." Kenniston went on to counsel a new alliance between the Americans of all ages, between youthful idealism and the "hard work, persistence, and dedication that has characterized the old culture."

This of course, will be well and good if the alliance is achieved through a mutual recognition by the generations of the human qualities found in both categories. Too often, some young people have assumed their own moral purity while treating those who did not agree with them as moral lepers. This attitude can only succeed in provoking a response of hostility, especially when the youth culture is decidedly vulnerable on a variety of charges ranging from impracticality to immorality.

In the last decade, our society has been shaken by adults who are so eager to acknowledge their own mistakes, that they overlook the inconsistencies and errors of those who criticize them. Young adults may find it difficult to trust those members of the older generation who preach morality and practice hypocrisy. But the remainder of the society in which we live should not have to pay their price by accepting the destructive, critical view of those who issue their non-negotiable demands, but who are immature to the extent of being unable to demonstrate a single shred of personal or social responsibility. If we recognize such Achilles' heels in the youthful armor of the revolutionaries, we will protect society in the long run.

True idealism does not blend with the youth cult. We can try to understand why many middle-aged adults are eager to link them in an ideal relationship. We don't like to think of the "kids" as they are: vulgar, crude, presumptuous, and spoiled. Their idealism does not justify such uncouth behavior. We are eager to follow the lead of columnist Ann Landers who says, "A generation that is against the Vietnam War, outspoken in behalf of equal opportunities for minority groups, dedicated to fighting pollution and saving our environment can't be all bad."

All bad. Precisely the point. Some of the unwashed dropouts may indeed have an interest in nature or in peaceful living. This does not deny that, despite their positive qualities, they negate the latter with their faults, which may be overpowering. The Ann Landers comment came in response to a concerned parent who had visited colleges, trying to evaluate them for a seventeen-year-old daughter. The parent described the "students" in their "dirty unisex clothing, unshaven, mop-haired males, braless girls in shawls, jeans, sandals and faded hiphuggers." Also obvious were lack of manners, dependence on obscenity, and the usual signs that the youth cult was thriving.

We want to tell ourselves that the "idealism" of "the kids" is really what matters. We want to forget that the youth cult is essentially a manifestation of parents' failure. Not the failure urged by those who seek to establish collective guilt! Not the failure to "understand" the kids! Instead, it is the product of the parents' (and teachers and government officials) decision to abrogate their responsibilities.

Why must one become a slob to understand idealism? What does drug addiction have to do with morality? Why do we pretend to see a relationship between the lessening of materialistic pressures (i.e., keeping up with the Joneses, trying to become the world's wealthiest man) and the exaltation of mediocrity (i.e., rock music, obscene poetry, illiterate literature, and "art" forms which require as a prerequisite total artistic incompetence)?

If the youth cult said, "Enjoy your work, or else find some work you can enjoy," and stopped there, we could not object. Too many citizens become caught up in the drive for power, the drive for wealth, and a mechanized routine of daily living. Pursuing one's own special talents or abilities is a fine idea. A redefinition of "success" is in order. We may well define success as the achievement of one's personal excellence in accordance with one's individual capabilities. If a man is a good father, or a woman is a good mother, they are "successful," according to this standard.

Examples of this redefinition are numerous. The classroom teacher becomes more concerned with teaching and working with his students than with achieving status distinctions on campus as a committee chairman. A businessman may find that his hobbies may be of an artistic nature. Perhaps his devotion to painting or writing or to studying nature may take time away from his work. If he spends his weekends with his family, instead of devoting that time to his office, his career may "suffer," but his life may be more meaningful.

Unfortunately, the youth cult doesn't stop there. It doesn't even begin there. Instead, it offers us the "new values" wrapped up in a package of slobbism. Redefinition of one's values is not only highly desirable, but often essential in today's technological society. But when a non-materialistic sense of values is linked with these other elements, which may be found at the very heart of the youth cult, the idealism becomes poisoned and perverted. We are offered not the joys of idyllic Utopia, but the primitive chaos of the Woodstock subculture.

. . . Distinguish between well-meaning idealism and ill-defined opportunism. A variety of self-seeking political militants often try to wrap themselves in the cloak of the New Politics. Consider what happened to George McGovern in his Presidential campaign. McGovern decided to depend on the New Left campaign organizers in order to launch his campaign for the nomination. Once he became the Democratic nominee, however, the chickens came home to roost. The "radiclib" element was ready to publicly embrace his candidacy, even though Democratic professionals realized that their endorsements would spell disaster. Jerry Rubin declared, "If McGovern is elected, he'll drop contempt charges against the Chicago Seven; I face five years in the can." Rubin and Chicago Seven attorney, William Kunstler, were both writing books about their pro-McGovern activities. An underground newspaper publisher called McGovern, "the presidential candidate with the Tim Leary smile." Leary himself endorsed McGovern, as did Eldridge Cleaver. Even Angela Davis tried to appear on McGovern rally platforms. Henry J. Taylor, diplomat and syndicated journalist, summed up the situation, declaring, "These militants are adult mobsters with coordinated plans and defined goals. Yet millions of every race, color, and creed in our country bitterly resent public officials who pamper this element and lack enough independence of it to push for laws that will safeguard the public from it."

Obviously, Senator McGovern did not share all the views of these extremists; but once he had established the alliance, he could not get rid of them. It is impossible to indulge in a mild flirtation with the political paranoids, the radicals of the New Left. Remember what happens to those who urge society to make allowances for riot and rebellion as youthful indiscretions, assuring us that everything will be all right after the revolution. Making concessions to political militants is a good way of poisoning the American system.

The alternative is to respond to the voices of radicalism with reason.

. . . Make decisions based upon your own conscience, not the collective guilt or conformity of others. Bertrand Russell, hardly a conservative, once remarked, "If fifty million people say a foolish thing, it is still a foolish thing." Peer-group pressure still proves itself capable of stampeding the public into behaving foolishly; people are always afraid of being different. A nation of sheep is a nation waiting for a hungry wolf. A young drug addict testified, "Kids today won't listen to parents, teachers, police, or anybody except their peers. Peer-group pressure is the only thing that is going to take the kids off drugs." The old truism, "If you can't beat them, join them" can prove disastrous in these present times of trial.

If you're going to take action, have a good reason, not just the excuse that everyone else is doing the same thing.

. . . Distinguish between liberalism and indulgence; draw distinctions between discipline and repression. Too often we have, in our zeal for tolerance, become indulgent. This lack of authority has been criticized by leading members of both political parties. Vice President Agnew criticized four major substitutes for discipline: the hero-villain lineup which assumes that the world is divided into good guys and bad guys; instant gratification, requiring immediate satisfaction of juvenile whims in order to demonstrate that the system is responsive; geneaphobia, the fear of the older generation as an anti-youth conspiracy; and the intellectual double standard. He emphasized his opposition to "shutting out views that oppose yours, because what you say is the revealed truth."

Frank S. Hogan, a leading Democrat and District Attorney of New York City for over thirty years, advised, "One of the saddest things in my experience is a definite decline in morality, to say nothing of the sins against life and property. The licentiousness, the filthiness of the motion picture, the underground press, so called, the theater—things that are accepted now." He went on to remind us, "Thus more and more young people say, 'It's the "in" thing. Nothing wrong with it. It is perfectly natural.' The same argument is made about drugs, especially marijuana."

Supreme Court Justice, Lewis F. Powell, levelled criticism against "doing your own thing" independent of the old-time disciplines of home, school, church, and community. He objected to an excessive tolerance of immoral conduct, and concluded, "I still believe that a sense of honor is necessary to personal self-respect; that duty, recognizing an individual subordination to community welfare, is as important as rights; that loyalty based on the trustworthiness of honorable men is still a virtue; and that work and self-discipline are as essential to individual happiness as they are to a viable society."

The views of these men are as applicable to our personal lives as they are toward our consciousness of political and social responsibility. Dr. James Anthony, director of child psychiatry at Washington University's school of medicine, has suggested that parents who are too permissive may cause painful confusion in their children.

We pride ourselves on being tolerant as human beings and as a society; this should continue. It would be a sad day for the United States if we became a nation with charity for none. But it will be an equally sad day for this nation if our zeal for tolerance renders us incapable of dealing with those political, social, and cultural challenges which can only be answered by a strong, firm hand.

. . . Evaluate our institutions on the basis of what they do accomplish rather than what they should accomplish. Don't conclude that an institution is obsolete because it isn't working. Our churches, for example, are suffering a variety of difficulties. A former drug addict, still a young girl, explained, "Churches aren't doing any good at all. They provide another recreation place where kids can sell drugs and get stoned." A friend of hers made similar observations about schools in which teachers permitted her to sleep when she came to school stoned on drugs. Police officers have seen a mockery made of justice, often by officers of the courts themselves. Court leniency in dealing with habitual offenders virtually has provoked a national scandal.

This does not mean that we should do away with our schools

and churches, abolish our courts, or turn society inside-out. We should not assume that institutions are working, simply because they are there; neither should we abolish those traditions or practices that are essential to a civilized society, simply because they have been mismanaged or allowed to decline in capability. District Attorney Cecil Hicks of Orange County (Calif.) says, "The gruesome crime just isn't shocking any more. People are exposed to it every day, in the newspapers, and particularly, on television, where it's so personal and immediate."

We must never allow a state of violence and terror to become a condition of normalcy; only by reasserting our belief in the traditional institutions that prevent violence, can we deal with these questions. Certainly, we should attend to the causes of violence as well as the aftereffects. But we must not confuse justice and mercy with bleeding-heart demagoguery.

. . . Regard high standards of ethics and morals as a source of pride, not something of which one must be ashamed. The debunking of excellence has become popular under the egalitarian ideal; in reality, it signifies a vicious distortion of that ideal. In the United States, equality of opportunity should depend upon exertion; we cannot afford an implied levelling process undertaken by the government or by self-styled social architects to reduce our social and economic hopes and aspirations toward the lowest common denominator. William S. Gilbert declared, "When everyone is somebody then no one's anybody."

The first step in the restoration of high ideals is the elimination of mediocrity as a personal standard. We have become dependent upon labels to convince us that tired, wornout rejections of responsibility are a panacea for our national ills. Henry F. Ottinger told his English class at the University of Missouri, "Ten years ago, the people around the fountains wore saddle shoes, chinos, and long hair. Now they're barefoot, wear army fatigues and have long hair. Big revelation: it's the same bunch of people."

Progress is splendid; too often we are not offered progress, only Marxism, anarchism, collectivism, or just plain teenage rebellion packaged under a new label.

. . . In making decisions about "the views of our children," make certain that all views are considered. No generation in history has had so many self-appointed spokesmen, so many representatives whose sole claim to authority is the decibel level of their voices. A host of campus organizations have arisen for purposes of opposing activities of the SDS and other campus radicals. The news media, however, have always devoted prime coverage to those movements which fit their own preconceived notion of student protest and youthful solidarity. Marijuana has been portrayed as a unifying force among the young, with its legalization inevitably years away. Yet marijuana use among adults has decreased, according to a 1973 survey, and opposition to its legalization is still overwhelming. A *Life* magazine poll of young Americans revealed that twenty percent considered themselves conservative, thirty-nine percent middle of the road, twenty-three percent liberal, against only five percent radical and thirteen percent undecided. Eighty-one percent said that their upbringing had been neither too strict nor too permissive; seventy-three percent agreed with their parents' values and ideals; eighty percent said that their parents had lived up to their own ideals.

The news media, and the journalistic profession in particular, have devoted too much attention to the views of some young people and portrayed them as the views of all young men and women. It isn't necessary to look for artificially created heroes. The Jerry Rubins and Jane Fondas would be insignificant, were they not glamorized and publicized by the press. The Charles Reichs would be revealed as apologists for a youth cult that never should have existed in the first place, if the academicians would lose their fears of being considered old-fashioned. The Alice Coopers would be regarded as social curiosities if they were not treated as serious artists. The uncouth, unwashed slobs would be recognized as leaders of a massive assault upon the public taste, if they were not welcomed into the homes and salons of the liberal élite that created radical chic.

The other young people are there, trying to make their voices heard. Often they fail to do so, not because their voices are drowned out by shouts of the crowd, but because society is so concerned with placating a small minority of dissenters that it fails to heed the concerns of its most responsible members.

. . . Revitalize the family as an American institution. Don't be fooled by prognosticators who want to substitute the commune or some other social unit. Remember that reform, like charity, still begins at home. If we're going to improve our society, we must start by improving ourselves.

As the whole is determined by the sum of its parts, so the nation is directed by the sum of its families. Each family represents America in microcosm. One of our primary goals *must* be the re-establishment of the home as a meaningful institution in American society.

James Hamilton, a nineteenth-century English clergyman, declared, "Six things are requisite to create a 'happy home.'" He went on to delineate these elements. "Integrity must be the architect, and tidiness the upholsterer. It must be warmed by affection, lighted up with cheerfulness; and industry must be the ventilator; renewing the atmosphere and bringing in fresh salubrity day by day; while over all as a protecting canopy and glory, nothing will suffice except the blessing of God."

These words may seem sentimental in our pseudo-sophisticated culture. But although times have changed, Hamilton's formula for a happy home still remains valid. Particularly in this period, when advocates of women's liberation are offering definitions of "home" which present a contrasting view, we must be certain of our standards.

We are told the home is a house, and that the family unit represents merely people who live in that house. Before many families achieved their present affluence, they were required by necessity to live and work together. If we reduce the concept of "family" or "home" to a series of tasks to be performed, we completely miss the true function of the home as an institution.

"Home" is not simply a place for washing, ironing, cooking, and sewing. Although these domestic activities have important roles in the home, the family must think further. Today a mother can often find substitutes for herself in washing or ironing; we need not suggest that she return to fulfill those functions by hand. But as the various household tasks continue to be delegated to machines or maids, a mother may easily assume that her maternal functions (i.e., keeping house) are being fulfilled. In turn, fathers may assume that their duties are essentially economical. As more and more mothers decide to "liberate" themselves, and join their "liberated" husbands, the family unit continues to suffer.

Families do not enjoy themselves together as they once did. Men and women are in more of a hurry today; they want to do more, faster, in less time. As they see the younger generation without any sense of direction, they would do well to remember that a man can live his life more slowly and still go further in the long run.

Today's fashionable solution to problems has been "communication." Presumably this means a dialogue between the generations. We tend to forget that a dialogue requires by definition that one party listen to another party. But "listening" does not mean that one party abandons ideals or principles in order to accommodate the other.

Too many members of the younger generation assume their own infallibility. They credit their own "youthful idealism"; they justify a flight toward folly. Too many members of the parental generation assume their own infallibility. If moral values are re-examined, young people must take the first step to maturity: they must recognize the hollow, superficial, and presumptuous aspects of the youth cult.

If some ostensibly mature parents refuse to acknowledge their own hypocrisies and inconsistencies, their errors are compounded by another group of adults. These men and women try to absolve their feelings of guilt by adopting meaningless slogans regarding "what the kids want."

Fathers and mothers must again become leaders at home! They must again put discipline, standards, and values in their proper perspective. Young men and women must eschew rebellion for its own sake and work for positive goals and constructive lives. Parents and children who lead separate lives together in the same house are not a family. Young men and women must remember that responsible reform leads to progress; irresponsible change leads only to disaster.

Family life should become a shared experience. Society should be oriented neither around the dollar nor an imaginary notion of perpetual youth. The home, for all its sentimental connotations, still represents the cornerstone of American life. Responsible men and women of all ages should join hands to reverse the trends which pervade society today. If parents and teachers had taken firm stands at the beginning, we would not be faced with a youth revolution which offers obscenity, slobbism, and drug addiction as its primary characteristics.

Such action does not imply an end to progress or an opposition to change. As we recognize the lack of a true sense of values in our society, we can begin to discover solutions. We are not in trouble because our values have been wrong, but because too many persons in both generations have displayed little concern for our values.

Many years ago, the celebrated poet, Goethe, remarked, "He is the happiest, be he king or peasant, who finds peace in his home." The passing years have not disproved his assertion. If the vanishing verdant forests disturb you, plant a tree! As the length of the work week decreases, families should have more time to live together and to enjoy their lives. Parents should distinguish between being martinets and being permissive; children should learn the difference between self-expression and an egocentric sense of self-importance. We cannot solve our problems by depending on tobacco, drugs, or psychiatrists. We cannot expect them to be solved for us by political candidates who promise to cure our national ills with huge financial giveaway programs. These difficulties did not start with money; they will not end because of it.

Instead, we must start at the bottom and work our way back to the top; we must begin, curiously enough at the beginning. These solutions may seem simple. A philosophical tome may be more impressive than a family picnic; an institution may appear to be more "modern" than a long talk between father and son or mother and daughter. Today's young men and women are often advised to strive constantly for independence, as if their relationships with their parents were business relationships determined by contract. Parents and children will have to face some hard truths about themselves. We will not solve our problems overnight. But we can begin. By restoring the family to its rightful place in society, we can take a first step on the long road back. We have seen the dismal result of a society in which parental leadership is abandoned and basic values are ignored in the name of "change" or "progress." The home should not be a point of departure, but a point of return. As our homes are revitalized, mature young men and women can assume the positions of leadership and responsibility denied them by the youth cult.

. . . Stand up and hear! Stand up to make yourself heard; a silent majority can stay silent for so long that when it is ready to make itself heard, the minority refuses to let the majority express its will. Hear what others say, but not only hear, listen! Don't feel compelled to apologize for your views because they seem old-fashioned or out-of-date. The nation will continue to flounder until we stop seeking the approval of a small, select corps of socio-political snobs. It is especially demanding for those with educational backgrounds to make their views known. Our society has come to mistakenly respect the verbal wizardry of the academe; a man can sound like a scholar and still think like a used-car salesman. Jargon is not insight.

In many ways, the 1960's were years of madness for our nation; our political upheavals, our social crises were often bizarre and distorted. We often attended the Mad Tea Party, with our values becoming sources of ridicule; our villains became heroes, our heroes became villains; our pride became our weakness; our weakness became our strength; our morals became our albatross, and our vices became our virtues.

But we can recover; we can rediscover those goals and values which have never really left us. They have been obscured by the skeptics, the snobs, the schemers, and the self–seekers; but they remain the cornerstone of the American tradition.

We are constantly in search of "new" solutions. We may be surprised to learn that the essential basis for constructive action has been with us all the time. But like the man who goes to church on Sunday and creates havoc the other six days of the week, we must renew our values and our ideals. Utopia may never exist, but we can discover new meaning in our lives by re-evaluating our sense of values together. This is the key. Values determine our goals and ideals. A society of standards, disciplines, and a moral renaissance is the only society that is really free. If we do not detour on the way, following the Pied Piper to the mythical land of Woodstock (and ensuing disaster), we may all find our way not to the youth cult, but to a mature and progressive reality.